The Fine Art of Copyediting

SECOND EDITION

Revised and Expanded

Including Advice to EDITORS on How to Get Along with AUTHORS
and Tips on Style for Both

Elsie Myers Stainton

COLUMBIA UNIVERSITY PRESS   NEW YORK

Columbia University Press
Publishers since 1893
New York   Chichester, West Sussex
Copyright © 2002 Columbia University Press
All rights reserved

Library of Congress Cataloging-in-Publication Data
Stainton, Elsie Myers, 1911–
     The fine art of copyediting / Elsie Myers Stainton. — 2nd ed.
        p.   cm.
     "Revised and expanded."
     Includes bibliographical references and index.
     ISBN 0–231–12478–3 (cloth) — ISBN 0–231–12479–1 (pbk.)
     1. Copy-reading.   I. Title.
     PN162 .S735   2002
808'.06607—dc21   2001028186

♾

Casebound editions of Columbia University Press books are
printed on permanent and durable acid-free paper.
Printed in the United States of America
c 10 9 8 7 6 5 4 3 2 1
p 10 9 8 7 6 5 4 3 2 1

The Fine Art of Copyediting

SECOND EDITION

For Helen and Jim, my children,
writers both, who stand upon the shoulders of their parents
to see far and accomplish much,

and for my
grandchildren—
Henry and Jake; Ian, Adam, and Sean—
the next generation

Time present and time past
Are both perhaps present in time future
And time future contained in time past.

—T. S. Eliot, "Burnt Norton," *Four Quartets*

Contents

Preface to the Second Edition

The first edition of this book aimed to give a concise yet comprehensive view of an editor's work and relations with authors and explained how the publishing process affects authors and editors. During the last decade, as nobody will deny, publishing procedures and editing techniques have changed beyond recall, and soon, possibly in the next decade, the old practice of creating typed manuscript pages, which are edited and then sent to a printer for typesetting, may become a vestige of the past. Publishers are now saying they will "consider accepting hard copy."

With this in mind, I have revised the chapters on editing procedures and computer techniques in depth. The chapter on handling proof has been altered, other sections have been updated, and a sample of computer-edited copy has been included. A new chapter, "The Fine Art," puts forth some learned-by-experience niceties of style, along with how-to-do-it advice. Additional information and more examples are included in the chapter "Notes, References, and Bibliographies." Finally, suggestions for achieving a first-rate index complete the update. And let us notice that a new point of view emerges—welcoming innovations, expecting more of them, honoring the speed made possible by electronic techniques, and appreciating the conveniences afforded by computer technology. This edition is longer than the first, with added index entries, but is guaranteed not to waste a word.

Authors now have extraordinary technological facilities for producing copy and for adding corrections and felicities to the text. The mechanical course of words from the head of an author to words on the pages of a book has been immeasurably simplified, while the headaches of editors involved in their part of the process have been considerably complicated. So throughout the text new suggestions are angled in to match the new technology. The challenge here has been to leave enough of the old so those hard-working noncomputerized authors and editors will feel they too are being helped. For convenience, the text of a book in progress is referred to as the "manuscript" whether it consists of typed pages or files on a computer diskette, unless of course the distinction is needed.

The copyeditor who knows what good prose looks and sounds like can truly help to improve a book. Hence I have added further pointers about noticing writing style—including sentence structure, modifiers, and punctuation. I take account of our ever-expanding vocabulary and the editor's responsibility to deal with it judiciously. And I've indulged myself by setting forth my considered attitude toward metaphors: it's a love-hate relationship. So now, at a later date in my life as an editor, I enjoy the pleasure of being companionable and confidential yet still hard-nosed.

I have revised and enlarged the "Annotated Bibliography" to accommodate new editions and new guides. A few old favorites appear, time-worn but still useful.

The most popular item in the old edition concerned nits, which remain as pesky as ever and as much in need of control.

Once again, my son, Jim, has furthered my endeavors, this time by dealing with the computer when it talked back to me (frequently). And my daughter, Helen, has been at the ready to plug the holes in my pronouncements and to open new avenues for me from her own experience.

Bernhard Kendler, ever-brilliant editor extraordinary of Cornell University Press, has added to this book refinements of expression that I particularly appreciate. Richard Rosenbaum, gifted Cornell designer and production manager, has contributed his skill and know-how to this enterprise, much to its benefit. And may I bow to Sarah St. Onge for improving my manuscript in all the ways a good copyeditor can.

The Fine Art of Copyediting

SECOND EDITION

Introduction

This guide is designed to tell enough about the publishing business for a would-be copyeditor to understand what must be done to prepare a manuscript for publication and why. Along with a brief overview of the profession and the opportunities it offers to editors, this handbook provides a manual of style and an outline of publishing procedures, as well as suggestions on where to find more information. It also addresses the unusual person-to-person problems in editing and aims to put its readers in the picture heading in the right direction.

My focus is on the editor's attitude toward the profession and on personal relations—editor to author and author to editor—those special nuances of human relations that can foul up the process of turning a manuscript into a good book. I offer practical advice on how to achieve mutual trust and respect and how to resolve the personal problems that good incisive editing can create. This slant other guides to the profession have overlooked.

I am picturing a college graduate who has majored in English, or history, or sociology, or journalism, or even biology and is thinking, "I'll bet I could be an editor; I wish I knew how."

I am thinking of a managing editor (I was one) who has just hired a novice editor and wishes (I know the feeling) that there were a little book that could get the new employee started and reduce the need for surveillance over the neophyte.

I see a freelance editor, alone with dictionaries and manuals, who needs some personal guidance on where to start and how far to go.

I sympathize with someone who has mastered the stylebooks and yet is puzzling over how much or how little to do with the manuscript at hand or wondering how to do what is needed in the time allotted.

I can call to mind an editor of some experience who would be happy to learn a few new tricks on both the personal and the professional levels.

And I know an old hand at editing who would enjoy finding new confirmation of some traditional ideas.

I've also encountered writers who need help with expressing their thoughts and wish for not a tome but just a guide covering the basics of grammar and a few pointers on style. Indeed, any author might also want to know something about the concerns of a publisher as well as how to write a book.

For all these people I have written this book.

ONE

Basics

Editors are everywhere. They are at work wherever words are being written and published—words about the universe, the world, our society, and our human sojourners here. Almost everybody thinks anybody can be an editor. Most editors think few can be good editors. Many good editors sometimes think nobody fully appreciates them. Yet any editor knows that many people have no literary skills, that some among them, quite a few in fact, appreciate what a good editor contributes.

THE COPYEDITOR'S JOB

What do copyeditors do? A copyeditor is assigned somebody else's words to work on and must pour effort and thought into making them literate and clear. Copyeditors may like or dislike, approve or disapprove of the subject matter, but it is their job to make improvements where improvements are due. These contradictions are familiar to copyeditors, most of whom are working for money, earning a living, and thus must apply their skills to the project before them.

Selflessness and anonymity are standard qualities for copyeditors; in the vineyard they are laborers whose names will not be on the wine bottle. Sometimes they would be pleased to own up to the vintage; other times they are glad to be unknown.

This abstract description of the job points up a fundamental aspect of the copyeditor's working life: one's own accomplishments are often counted by readers as belonging to the author. From this point of view the editing process may be thought to pose a moral dilemma. Consider an extreme case: a manuscript that has been submitted to a publisher puts forth an appealing idea; it is timely; many readers might be interested in it. But the author has few literary gifts, often misstates the case, and expresses ideas tonelessly. So the manuscript is accepted, and in this unusual instance a copyeditor employed by the publishing house goes to work on it—revises many sentences, changes the order of the parts, deletes repetitious sections, and so on. The gem of an idea is now mounted in a suitable setting. The author, in the preface of the book, graciously thanks the publisher's staff, perhaps even naming the copyeditor in question, for many improvements. (The faults that remain, the preface says, are attributable of course to the author alone.) Is the presentation of this book as the work of its author morally right? The author has had a lot of help.

We in the profession generally say, so be it. Many authors need help; most publishers see one of their roles as supplying it.

THE COPYEDITOR'S STANCE

What kind of person is this, who works behind the scenes, greases someone else's axle?

The good copyeditor, above all, is a fusspot—one who cares. This is not to say that other workers do not care. They have their cares. In the arena of writing, the editor cares about honest expression, about order, about clarity, and about logic. Copyeditors hate non sequiturs and arguments ad hominem, ambiguities and muddy thinking, inconsistencies and badly proportioned parts, jargon, cant, and gobbledygook. They believe that commas and semicolons matter, that spelling a word correctly is important. And they are pleased to help.

The copyeditor's approach, then, begins with "I care"—about the words, sentences, and paragraphs in the articles, pamphlets, and books that are helped along toward publication. The editor's charge is to make sure that the words written will be comprehensible to those who read them. Communication. No small aim.

In this light, it seems reasonable that editors need to develop a working enthusiasm for the ideas they are dealing with. The good editor tries to make a murky idea clear and to make sure a brilliant idea sparkles. The professional editor tries to help any author to say what is meant and of course hopes that the author then means what has been said.

KINDS OF EDITORS

Various editors may deal with manuscripts at different stages of the publishing process depending on the procedures at a publishing house. A procurement, or acquisitions, editor searches out the manuscript on behalf of the publisher. A production editor may handle the manuscript from the signing of a contract to publish it through to production, including copyediting and checking proof, or may refer it at one point to a copyeditor for detailed scrutiny. An executive editor often finds and helps to develop a new work; such editors sometimes keep a close watch over the product from start to finish. At some publishers one person may wear several of these hats. A managing editor usually oversees the copyeditors in an editing department. A copyeditor closely reads and carefully corrects the manuscript, word by word, character by character straight through.

THE VALUE OF COPYEDITING

Copyediting adds to the cost of publishing. So questions arise: Why bother? Printing costs are inescapable, but can't copyediting costs be reduced or eliminated? How much is gained by enhancing the text, how much in sales, in prestige, in general good?

Copyeditors can easily point to improvements: they make texts grammatically correct, clearer, easier to read, and more to the point. Publishers, though, generally supply guidelines to their editors as to how much editing is feasible—affordable—in view of the probable sales of a book. The greater the projected sales, the more money for editing if more editing is going to mean more sales. The publisher is lucky when a potentially popular item requires little editing. Considerable fine-line judgment is called for when a worthy project shows up that needs heavy editing yet will not reward the publisher with heavy sales. Then the copyeditor must make the text passable but will not spend the time, which costs money, to do everything possible. This kind of editing is not necessarily the easiest, because judgment must be exercised continuously. In publishing houses, the degree of necessary editing is usually determined in advance and stipulated for the editor as minimal, routine, or heavy. The publisher, as the cost-conscious head of a business, must decide how much editing time—money—can reasonably go into the production of a book so as to break even or make a profit.

With this important practical proviso in mind, copyeditors do their best to make any manuscript better. Who gains thereby?

First, the publisher gains. No firm is respected if its books contain misspellings or grammatical errors or if reviewers cite incomprehensible passages or ideas. So a publishing house is protecting its reputation by relying on editors.

Authors are saved from revealing their own foibles and shortcomings. Their reputations are enhanced, and perhaps each learns something during the editing process. The next book will be better.

Readers too are blessed when they are not distracted by misspellings or confused by ambiguities and instead may be charmed by felicitous expressions and enlightened by brilliant ideas.

Finally, copyeditors are also rewarded, by the knowledge that something faulty was made acceptable, something good made better, and something very good made extraordinary. This knowledge translates into satisfaction. The profession of copyediting pays its way, is worth a place in the sun. With this in mind, an editor may achieve an appropriate, optimistic attitude toward the profession—and toward the files in the computer or the manuscript on the desk.

TWO

Legal and Contractual Aspects
of Publishing

In the long process of producing a book, who is responsible for what? A copyeditor who has spent many hours on a manuscript begins to have a proprietary interest in it. The copyeditor is supposed to catch any errors in the piece, is expected to notice that the name of Georges Clemenceau is misspelled, that Charles Darwin is placed in the wrong century, that a discussion of D. H. Lawrence lacks any mention of sex, that the generalizations about birth control from six examples are unreliable. With such responsibilities, this editor tends to think of the manuscript as his or her own. Whose is it?

MUTUAL DEPENDENCY

In part the manuscript belongs to the publisher, who has contracted to put money into it and staked reputation and financial resources on it. Yet it is the author's brainchild: without the author, no book. A mutual dependency exists, but it is possible to distinguish what is whose.

The copyeditor must remember that the author's name goes on the title page and that it is the author who must stand by what is said on the pages following. Therefore the book is the author's. The author is boss except in a few matters: in some important legal areas, as in the case of libel, and in most production decisions, such as design, for which the publisher is generally responsible.

LIBEL

Legally and practically the publisher—and, acting for the publisher, the copyeditor—is obliged to be alert for possible libel. Although the contract signed by the author supposedly guarantees the publisher that the manuscript contains no libelous material, suits for libel are directed at both author and publisher. Hence the copyeditor must be the publisher's watchdog, alert for possible derogatory, purposefully harmful statements made about living people or, in the unusual case, about a dead person if descendants could claim consequent willful injury to themselves.

The problem of libel does not show up often, but when it does, it is serious. One fine manuscript about pre–World War II Communists in the United States had to be scrapped because the author refused to delete the names of certain people listed as members of Communist-front organizations. The copyeditor signaled the problem, and a lawyer engaged by the publisher to vet the manuscript (examine it for libel) declared that the people named could sue for libel and probably would, being litigious types. The expense and effort involved in attempting to prove the accuracy of the statements, a traditional defense against a claim of libel, were a price that the press decided it could not afford, although the interests of truth and justice might have been served thereby. Most publishers would make the same decision in such a circumstance.

In another case an author included a derogatory account, based on oral descriptions given him by persons claiming to be witnesses, of an incident involving a traveler in Africa. The traveler declared that the account in the book was libelous and threatened suit. The case was resolved out of court by the publisher's agreeing to print a public retraction and to alter the supposedly libelous statements in all copies of the book still in stock.

Here a more careful check of sources, and particularly identification and attribution of the source for the story, might have saved the author and the publisher embarrassment, but any derogatory, possibly damaging statement deserves a copyeditor's careful scrutiny—of both the author's intent and the reliability of the sources.

INDISCRETION (BIAS)

What may be called indiscretion is not so serious as libel. Court action is not likely to result from it. But an injudicious remark may cause whole classes of potential readers to become alienated, mistrustful of the author, inclined to dismiss the book, or determined to criticize the author and publisher. Here we need to explore the area of biased language—a delicate, important, and ever-changing problem in our society.

In a book of articles by various authors, one author, an Anglican, took a nasty sideswipe at Catholics. This dig should have been eliminated, since it was tangential to, really distracting from, the general argument and would alienate readers who might otherwise be interested in the author's thesis. There is of course no harm in indicating one's own religious belief, but it is sensible to be tolerant in print. The Anglican professor was adamant. Later, a reviewer struck out at this very comment, thus damaging the potential of an entire book because of a single sentence.

This suggestion is not meant to advocate disguising wolves in sheepskins. Writers must not be advised to conceal their points of view; rather, they should be encouraged to state clearly their personal position or bias, when relevant. What the copyeditor eliminates are tangential, irrelevant slurs that may arouse a reader's distrust needlessly. It is surprising how many of these show up in manuscripts.

On another front sexism is deplored by a large constituency of potential readers. An author may flaunt his masculine qualities if he pleases. More frequently, however, missteps are taken unwittingly, vestiges of former attitudes:

The forklift operator, a woman, was unable to control the jammed gears.

Here mention of the gender of the operator should be removed, since it suggests that a man could have controlled the machine.

Avoiding sexual slurs or unwitting sexual slights requires a sensitive mindset and an alert reading of changing attitudes and language. But a tolerant stance on sexual orientation in all its aspects is required of a copyeditor on the job. Much help on currently acceptable language is to be found in recent manuals of style and especially in books such as Miller and Swift's *Handbook of Nonsexist Writing*. The AAUP *Guidelines for Bias-Free Writing* goes further in this direction to supply appropriate language for terms that are objectionable to readers with same-sex or bisexual orientation.

Racial prejudices persist. Despite much goodwill and well-meaning effort, subtle assumptions continue. A copyeditor should watch for this problem and alert authors to it:

The poor black Haitians did not understand the suggestions of the sociologists.

That the Haitians were black is irrelevant. The editor should delete "black" and let the Haitians be people of any complexion like the sociologists. In another context, that the Haitians were black might be relevant.

This and similar so-called indiscretions can be labeled intolerance or bias. But promoting tolerance is hardly the copyeditor's purview, so why bring it up? Because the editor always has in mind the readership of the article or book, as indeed the author should. Let's not discourage or offend readers needlessly. Gratuitous jabs leave blemishes the copyeditor should try to remove. (Specific suggestions on achieving bias-free writing are put forward under that subheading in Chapter 7, "A Concise Manual of Writing Style for Copyeditors.")

In all these questions, copyeditors are expected to exercise judgment and tact. No wonder, after scores if not hundreds of decisions in the course of editing a manuscript, that they may feel somewhat proprietorial.

COPYRIGHT AND PERMISSIONS

The contract, or memorandum of agreement, is customarily a standard printed form supplied by the publisher: the publisher agrees to publish and pay royalties; the author agrees to deliver a manuscript and follow through on proofreading and indexing. The copyeditor needs to be concerned with only certain aspects of this agreement.

One important task is to check that the author has obtained permission to quote from copyrighted sources. The author, by contract, guarantees that (as in one publisher's memorandum of agreement) "said work does not infringe any copyright or violate any property rights" and "agrees to secure at his/her own expense the necessary permissions to reprint excerpts and/or illustrations to be included in the work." The copyeditor must try to make sure that the author observes this agreement, for infringement of copyright is serious and may be grounds for legal action or serve to damage the author's and the publisher's reputation.

Permission must be obtained from the publisher for quotations from a publication beyond what is considered "fair use" and must be acknowledged with an appropriate or sometimes a stipulated credit line. Quoting a few paragraphs of prose or a few lines of poetry normally is considered "fair use." But permission is needed to use a long excerpt or an accumulation of briefer excerpts in prose, a whole poem or sometimes only ten or twelve lines of poetry, and any table, chart, or figure. The copyeditor must check, if another editor has not already done so, that all permissions and acknowledgments are in order and must have in hand all permissions and acknowledgments before typesetting begins.

Plagiarism—the use of unauthorized, unacknowledged material—is in a class with stealing, as any author should know. The editor might well make sure that an author understands the import of the copyright laws.

DESIGN

A copyeditor needs to know if the contract says something like: "All details as to the manner of publication, production, and promotion, including the title, selling price, and number and destination of free copies, shall be left to the sole discretion of the publisher."

The customary proviso in the contract specifying that design and production are at the discretion of the publishing house is necessary because the publisher needs to control the amount of money to be expended on any one book. Experienced designers are skilled in getting the most for that money. The author too should rely on these designers. But many authors have notions about the design of their books. These notions are not all bad. The prudent publisher will usually consider them and might adopt them, maybe in modified form. Trouble comes when an author has lived with a notion, say a title, for so long that any alteration appears to be sacrilege—like changing the name of an infant after the christening. In such a case, the editor may have to cite, diplomatically, all the reasons against the questionable book title and perhaps ask for assistance from colleagues in sales, who can marshal effective practical arguments.

Illustrations

When illustrations (charts, diagrams, drawings, etc.) are to be included in a book, the publisher usually expects the author to furnish final, camera-ready copy, and the copyeditor may have to ask the author to revise if necessary (as when the symbols in a chart do not match those used throughout the text). Sometimes small alterations can be made by the production department; the editor consults with production staff about any such questions.

Similarly it is usually the author's responsibility to provide photographs suitable for reproduction and the editor's job to consider their quality and appropriateness, with the designer's help.

Jackets

Sometimes it falls to a managing or executive editor to justify a dust jacket design to an author who is unhappy with it. One author who had chosen a metaphorical title for his book unexpectedly insisted that the metaphor must not be used in the design. Unfortunately he did not express that wish until long after the jacket was under way. It was then necessary to explain that jackets are printed early since sales staff show them to wholesalers and at bookstores even before the book is published. So this author's initial joy at handling a copy of his book was mingled with dismay at beholding pictured there a literal rendering of the title *Pillars of Ice* (the title has been changed to protect the guilty). But we can forgive a publisher's artist who, with no directions to the contrary, chose to embody a lively metaphor in the artwork.

The jacket of a book is considered advertising and is generally outside the purview of the copyeditor. Sales and advertising personnel decide which aspects of the book to put forward so as to claim the attention of book buyers—and browsers or passersby—a point of view quite dissimilar from that of most editors.

OTHER CONTRACTUAL SPECIFICS

Titles

The difficulty with *Pillars of Ice* goes deeper than the jacket-design squabble. Not a clue to the book's subject is given in that title. Such a vague uninformative label is worthless for sales and advertising, and the editor might well try to dissuade an author from holding on to it. The contract usually mentions the title as "tentative," anticipating a change.

The title of a book is its special tag, its distinguishing label. The choice of words is limited only by the number of words in the English language (and not even that), yet how few of them show up in titles. An earlier generation was fond of *Nature* and *Patterns*; *Study* has long been favored; *Vision*, *Structure*, and *Stance* have had a vogue. Popular, fashionable words have the advantage of telegraphing meanings to those in the know, hence use of them is justified in titles, which must tell much in brief space. Esoteric terms are not useful. Although generality is needed vagueness is not, and the poetic use of words in a title, except for poetry and fiction, may be confusing to potential readers and damaging to possible sales. If a metaphor is used, let it be linked to the theme of the book. A catchall main title that requires a subtitle is bad. No question about it, it's bad:

Vision and Response: A Study in Optics

Vision and Response: Case Studies in the Motor Control of Disturbed Children

Vision and Response: The Perception by Rhesus Monkeys of Color-Coded Commands

Vision and Response: The Mormon Trek Westward

Vision and Response: Advances in Agricultural Development

Vision and Response: A Comparison of Old and New Testament Attitudes Toward Revelation

Vision and Response: The Genius of Salvador Dali

Vision and Response: What the Honey Bee Can See and What He Does About It

Vision and Response: A Case Study in Urban Renewal

Vision and Response: Milton's Apocalyptic Genius

Vision and Response: Browning's Rhetorical Stance

Since keyword searches are now the primary means of finding books in library catalogs and in bookstore listings on the Internet, a lively, informative key word or phrase is extremely useful. If the author can't come up with this carrot, the staff of the press might try to supply it.

I know of two instances where the publisher helped: my son's *Afraid of the Dark* (a metaphor that works), subtitled *What Whites and Blacks Need to Know About Each Other*; and *The Fine Art of Copyediting* (herewith).

Proofs and AAs

The contract also spells out the author's responsibility to read proof and to pay for excess author's alterations (AAs or aa's) in proof. The contract may read somewhat as follows:

> The author agrees to read, correct, and return promptly all proofs of the work. If the author shall make or cause to be made any alterations in type, illustrations, or in plates, other than those resulting from printer's errors (PEs or pe's), that shall exceed [5 or 10] percent of the cost of original composition, the expense of such alterations shall be borne by the author. In the interest of assuring prompt publication of the work, the publisher shall have the right to reject any alterations, other than typographical errors or correction of factual errors.

Index

A good book deserves a good index. Here again the contract normally specifies that the index shall be compiled by the author or, if not by the author, by a freelancer at the author's expense.

So in general the publisher is responsible for providing sensible editing, suitable design and packaging, and appropriate sales promotion and effective distribution. The author is responsible for the ideas put forth, the method of presentation, and the style of writing, as well as the accuracy and cogency of the material. The copyeditor works for both publisher and author to produce, as far as possible, a better book.

THREE

Types of Editing

The basics are the same for most types of editing. The copyeditor corrects spelling, grammar, and punctuation, removes ambiguities and obscurities, and also may consider the proportion of the parts—in books and pamphlets, in articles for dictionaries and encyclopedias, or in items for journals and newspapers. In any of these, the writing must be accurate, clear, consistent, and concise, and the copyeditor must consider costs of production, legal aspects, and readership. The copyeditor also flags for design and composition special elements in the manuscript, such as extracts, unusual type, and levels of headings. Along the way, illustrative material must be checked and cued to the text.

BOOKS

Book manuscripts early on can be defined according to their market: trade, scholarly, textbook, reference. A trade book appeals to a general audience and is sold in commercial bookstores. A scholarly book is aimed at specialists who know the field well, and it will be sold in university and specialized bookstores and to libraries. A textbook is for students and usually sold through public-school channels or at university and college bookstores. A reference book can be for general readers or specialists, and it too is sold through bookstores and to libraries.

According to the way the acquisitions/executive editor or sales department has defined the book, the copyeditor knows from the start what is expected of a manuscript. The kind and extent of the specific editing depend on the condition of the manuscript and the requirements of the readers for whom it is designed, as well as on the organization of responsibilities in the publishing house.

The copyeditor scrutinizes every word and mark of punctuation, making the last detailed check of the text before it is set in type, after which changes are prohibitively expensive. This editor may or may not be in touch with the author. More often than not he or she is a freelancer working outside the publisher's offices.

For some publishing houses this detailed check for errors is all the copyeditor does; another editor may have examined the manuscript for ambiguities or lapses, considered its length and the proportion of the parts, and communicated with the author. In other houses, this consideration of the overall plan and execution falls to the copyeditor. In each organization, the respective responsibilities are made clear.

Copyeditors of books are relatively free to use their own judgment and to consider the author's wishes on matters of style. For volumes in a series, though, where conformity is desirable throughout, the publisher will impose a uniform style to be followed in all such matters as punctuation, spelling, and usage.

Publishers also may have a collection of precepts for editors called house style. These precepts pertain to rules such as using or omitting a comma in a series before *and* or to marking such acronyms as NATO for small capitals. (When the acronym comes at the beginning of a sentence, the editor might well recast the sentence so as to avoid the oddity of starting a sentence with a small capital.)

Having a house style for all the books produced in a publishing house makes editing easier: if the formal aspects are all handled in the same way, any editor can work on any manuscript at any stage without introducing inconsistencies. For most books, however, the restrictions of a particular house style are unnecessary, although the discipline of the subject, such as law or medicine or chemistry, may have its own conventions.

Trade Books

Trade books are for the general reading public or for a special segment of that public. Trade books generally should be self-explanatory and should not require readers to have information beyond what appears in the book itself.

The editors of nonfiction trade books at commercial houses and at university presses have essentially the same task: to make the text readable and usually to code the manuscript for design. In commercial houses work on nonfiction books ranges from minimal editing (correcting spelling and coding long quotations and poetry for design) to major rewriting and corrective surgery.

If in some commercial houses copyeditors generally offer fewer suggestions than university press editors, as I hear from a number of American authors who have had experience at both levels, perhaps the reason is that scholarly presses may work with a greater number of first-time authors, who need more help. Most authors who publish with commercial houses are professional writers.

Commercial publishers offer subcategories of trade books that usually include poetry, children's books, and fiction. A few university presses also publish poetry and fiction.

The copyeditor of fiction, in addition to a knowledge of basics, needs to appreciate the author's aims; in this kind of editing there is room for intuition and for a sense of what the writer is trying to say. The novelist is happy to comply with a suggestion that a touch more is needed at the end or that a character not mentioned for fifty pages needs to be reintroduced. Some famous novelists have continued with a publisher because of a copyeditor there.

The editing of fiction, once the book is accepted, tends to be lighter than that of nonfiction, although it can be very heavy, both structural and detailed. In fiction, anachronisms need to be eliminated, and the sequence of time and events needs to be checked. Some larger publishers of fiction give much editorial advice in advance before acceptance, or a literary agent may give invaluable guidance on storyline, characters, and so on beforehand.

Scholarly Books

Scholarly books, sometimes called "short-discount" books (for which booksellers receive a smaller percentage off the retail price than is allowed on trade books), are directed toward specific, specialist readerships. Scholarly books almost without exception include notes and bibliography, and it is expected that these books might be difficult reading for the uninformed. In the copyediting, customary usage among similar scholars is observed. Sociologists and anthropologists, historians and economists, literary critics, scientists of all branches—each has a preferred form for notes or references and bibliography, and all have guidelines for the editor to use.

The university publisher might be happy to sell fifteen hundred copies. Commercial houses also publish scholarly books, but only those expected to have wide appeal and strong sales.

Textbooks

Textbooks are for students and are usually designed for a specific course or courses. Textbooks may contain special sections such as reading assignments, suggestions for further reading, and questions for the student.

University press textbooks sometimes have a more durable sales history than the short-discount books from these presses; they may continue to make money for the publisher until another edition is ready. Some venerated university press textbooks are the bread-and-butter items on the publisher's list, selling several thousands year after year.

Commercial houses specializing in textbooks usually print in much larger quantities and will be disappointed if their books don't sell many thousands of copies each year. In the large houses that aim to develop textbook series to be used nationwide, a corps of editors is required at several levels as well as a fleet of salespeople.

Even for a single text, several editors may be involved: after the acquisitions editor there may come a developmental editor, who works with the author on the overall point of view in the manuscript, on style, and on coverage of the subject. That editor will constantly compare the textbook with competing books by other publishers to make sure the book is competitive. Then the copyeditor (not necessarily a specialist on the subject of the book) works on sense, grammar, and style. In the larger companies, these copyeditors usually do not deal with the author, although in smaller houses they might. After copyediting, if the text is in mathematics, for example, including problems for illustration or for the student to solve, a solver comes into the picture to check that the mathematical problems are correctly handled.

When a textbook is part of a series to be used across the United States, a small team of editors may cooperate under the acquisitions (or developmental) editor. And correlation editors check the various state curriculum requirements and prepare pamphlets for each state, showing how the text meets state requirements.

The everyday, all-purpose, experienced copyeditor can do well with trade books, scholarly works, or textbooks on almost any subject, but mathematics, physics, chemistry, medicine, and the like also require a specialist editor to check and to style equations and formulas and, for example, to tell the printer where to break formulas or equations that run over a line or two.

Scientific and Professional Books

The many scientific books and specialized books for people in other professions, such as business, law, or medicine, are not exactly trade books, textbooks, or scholarly books. These professional books disseminate detailed information about expanding technologies—in medicine, chemistry, physics, engineering, veterinary science, pharmacology, what have you. The editors of these volumes must have detailed knowledge of usage in the field. The competent editor who also has training in math, science, or economics is in demand and indeed is well paid.

But here accuracy of every detail is all-important: place a decimal point incorrectly in a dosage, and a patient could die.

REFERENCE VOLUMES

Reference books, including dictionaries and encyclopedias, form another large category. They may be designed for the general public, an extremely wide market, as the standard dictionaries and almanacs are, or for the specialist, as *The Oxford Classical Dictionary*.

Dictionaries of the English Language

Each of our great dictionaries of the English language has a staff of editors who search current publications in order to find new words, new usages, and other changes in the language, and these editors will tell you that the English language is constantly changing. (The average copyeditor must keep this in mind and must turn for help to the latest dictionary.)

Other Dictionaries and Encyclopedias

There are also many encyclopedic dictionaries, such as the *Dictionary of American Writers* and *The New Grove Dictionary of Music and Musicians*, usually in multiple volumes.

Copyediting of these works is exacting and, indeed, crucial. The editors will take material written by perhaps hundreds or even thousands of contributors and reform it into a homogeneous, consistent reference work, designed for the general reading public.

The biggest job usually is to refashion the raw material provided by contributors into concise dictionary format, for although the many authors will have been given advance guidelines in considerable detail, few will have followed the given format. Some authors will have omitted essential information such as locales or dates. These one of the editors will supply. Other authors will have included irrelevant material or more information than is feasible for a reference work. This an editor will remove.

These editors generally are free to revise or rewrite extensively as the need may be. The authors may see proof, but they usually do not have the final say because the requirements of the huge project override the preferences of individual contributors. The pieces are commissioned by, and become the property of, the publisher.

The editing of a comprehensive general encyclopedia or dictionary has to be supervised and coordinated, so the copyeditors engaged in such a large project will find themselves on a team. Cooperation is required in a way hardly ever to be found in book editing. Several editors will review the articles, each scrutinizing specific details, all referring to a huge "bible" of guidelines. The many facts will be checked. Variant spellings of names will be noted at appropriate places in the text, but a standard form will be chosen for use throughout. Indexes and cross-references will be compiled. Sometimes, with editing upon editing, the problem of having too many cooks must be resolved. Common sense is in great demand, as is attention to detail.

The readership for these volumes is enormous, and the books will be used for decades. Their contribution, in the convenient assemblage of related facts, is indeed great.

MISCELLANEOUS

Many writers and editors are needed for government reports, public information pamphlets, project summaries, and the like. Corporations too publish booklets, directions for the use of their products, and other information that could be classified as public relations or advertising. The computer industry is turning out books of instructions. We are surrounded by printed matter.

Here the knowledgeable editor can contribute much—by getting rid of pomposity and jargon, by striking out unnecessary words and circumlocutions, and by concentrating on the citizen's or consumer's need to know. Everybody needs straight talk.

JOURNALS

Popular magazines for the mass market have their own guidelines for editors and their own notions about reaching their constituencies.

Innumerable other periodicals, devoted to every subject imaginable, also employ editors. For articles in these periodicals, an overall style, or house style, will have been predetermined in order to achieve uniformity throughout the publication and has to be followed by authors and editors. This necessity makes an editor's life easier in one respect, because fewer decisions have to be considered. Journals establish their own style in using the series comma with *and*, in preferring certain capitalization and italics, in citing names and titles, and in the form of notes and references, including abbreviations.

Often too the copyeditor of journal articles has less freedom to revise extensively. The articles customarily have been approved by members of an editorial board, who may have suggested changes earlier and who do not reread the manuscripts after editing. Nevertheless, you, as copyeditor, can accomplish much in these circumstances with small improvements rather than wholesale changes. Like the restrictions a poet faces in writing a sonnet, limitations sometimes contribute to the success of an effort.

Journals, the copyeditor must keep in mind, are published on a regular schedule. The June issue of a quarterly may have to be in the warehouse, ready to be posted to subscribers, by May 15. Its editing may have to be completed in January. Indeed the manuscript for June may be in the house for editing while the proof for March is also in house being checked. The editor then must fit all the work into the time allotted.

The newspaper business is a world apart, with its own guidelines, traditions, preparatory schools, pressures, and excitement. Newspaper editors must know how to spell and be aware of the latest usage; how to punctuate using *The Associated Press Stylebook* (or the newspaper's own guidelines); how to write, condense, and expand; and how to work under tight deadlines. Some editors are also required to write headlines and subheadings. And newspaper editors must always be alert to catch any omissions or slipups, factual or judgmental, in their paper's presentation of the news.

Publishing is big business. The decision to publish anything involves educated guesswork—a gamble. Editors can help to make the gamble less risky.

FOUR

The Editor's Dilemma

How can one point out faults graciously?

Some of a copyeditor's success depends on personal relations. To do a really good job on a manuscript, an editor needs to be on good terms with the author, even though mostly at a distance.

Editing a manuscript involves more than dealing with words on paper; it concerns working with a human being who is revealing an important part of himself or herself to the public. The author may have spent years on this manuscript. It may have called for sacrifices from family members; it surely has cost money, physical and mental effort, even anguish. A professional reputation may be at stake. In this relationship, editor to author, person to person, no help can be found in manuals of style. The editor must turn from the dictionaries and manuals to look at what is happening: an untried, tender, vulnerable brainchild is being offered to the world for approval. An author may be confident, resolute, worried, or fearful or, worse, bellicose, argumentative, vacillating, or timid. Whether the author is composed or nervous, the best approach for the editor is to be kind, to look for the good in the manuscript.

PERSONAL RELATIONS

William Strunk Jr. used to tell a story about William Lyon Phelps, of Yale, who was an accomplished lecturer. The morning after one of his lectures, Professor Phelps was taking his customary walk along the streets of New Haven when he was accosted by a tiny, elderly woman.

"Oh, Professor Phelps," she said, "your talk last night was just wonderful! I did so enjoy it." And then she added, "But after all you probably don't care about comments from somebody like little old me."

Professor Phelps paused, removed his hat, and bowed. "Madam," he said, "I am a glutton for praise."

Praise

Taking account that authors, like editors, are only human, remember that authors doubtless have an appetite for praise and that relations with them can be improved by dishing up some honest compliments or at least some words of appreciation, along with corrections, revisions, and queries.

Picture a relationship where one person points out misspelled words, faulty grammar, obscure passages, and repetition in another's work. It takes an unusual person to enjoy, or even tolerate, the heaped-up criticisms—exactly what a good copyeditor contributes. If the author says, "You are right; I am wrong," and changes everything as suggested, you may be pleased. If the author says, "I'm right; you're wrong," and won't change anything, you are in trouble. Either way the exchange does not give hope of the kind of give-and-take that often results in great improvements. But when a copyeditor's suggestion strikes home and sparks an even better revision by the author, the best kind of cooperation is taking place. So win over your author with a sympathetic approach, pleasantly authoritative but not hidebound. You have your press behind you and all the dictionaries and manuals of style. Now you need only the cooperation of this one practitioner.

Sometime during the editing the author must come to trust you if efforts to improve the manuscript are to succeed. Important in this mix is your appreciation of the author's efforts and confirmation that your aims are the same as the author's: to produce a first-rate book.

Differences of Opinion

When I was managing editor at Cornell University Press, I frequently got calls from professors at Cornell who felt they were being mistreated by a copyeditor at another publisher. They always were excited, ready to defend their prose. What could I do?

I tried to remain on both sides of the controversy. This editor, this publisher, I said, is doing a job and is trying to be helpful, so first examine the suggestions to discover whether there is any good in them; then at least express your views and get an answer. (I always hoped I was not defending an inexperienced editor somewhere.) "If necessary," I told my faculty friends, "you may feel you must say: 'No, thanks,' with thanks." The choice may or may not be a big deal, depending on whether at that stage it costs money.

In cases such as these, the editor somewhere might have made better headway by giving early on the reasons for changes in style. Indeed an editor must be ready to cite a rule or usage for every editing change on the manuscript.

William Safire defended in print a friend who fell out with an editor over hyphens. "Let's kill all the copyeditors," Safire said. Closed-up or hyphenated? Copyeditors, there's an argument not worth fighting about, for there is no misunderstanding over what you're referring to when you write "worth-while" or "worthwhile," "world-view" or "worldview." Similar confrontations show up over capitalization. Upper or lower case? "Chapter 7" or "chapter 7," "Fig. 3" or "fig. 3"? If a specific chapter or figure in a specific book is *something*, then as the *name of something* it deserves caps, consistently. But authorities disagree on this distinction, and the arguments are cogent on both sides—e e cummings survived. So the copyeditor's burden is to accept somebody's command and be consistent. I would accept an author's choice in this regard, but the editor who strongly favors otherwise or is constrained by house rules might well offer to the author strong reasons for the choice. To make the distinction clearer, notice that "line 2" and "paragraph 3" do not qualify as names of something. But this squabble is not worth an argument. Communication, understanding, informing, consistency—these are our business. Argue if you must over consistency, the choice of words, the use of adverbs and adjectives, vague statements, the meaning—there's where editors can make a difference.

DIFFICULT MANUSCRIPTS

Sometimes it is not easy for a copyeditor to see the good in a manuscript. Some manuscripts seem sloppily prepared, inane, or both. Then you have to believe that the decision to publish was made responsibly, that any manuscript on the way to being published deserves careful editing, that there must be something valuable in this one.

Editors' Ploys

Suppose a manuscript seems to belabor perfectly obvious arguments, hashing over points long since resolved. You can comment: "Most of your readers will agree with you." And then add: "But maybe you should try to give your argument a new twist."

Suppose the manuscript is full of muddled ideas: the author hasn't made points clear. You can comment: "You have tackled a very difficult subject." The author will take this as praise and may then be open to your specific suggestions.

Suppose that after making many small but painstaking corrections and improvements, you receive the manuscript back with a huge black comment scribbled on it: "Nit-picking!" What to do? Respond neatly somewhere for the author to see but marked not to be set in type: "But who wants nits?"

The Confident Bad Writer

The confident, assertive, bad writer presents one of the toughest problems an acquisitions editor or a copyeditor has to face. What to do? First praise the manuscript. There must be something to praise: its originality, its contribution, its unique point of view, its interesting theme, something. Pseudo praise won't do; a good must be singled out for enthusiastic comment. This may be done by letter if you are in touch with the author, if not by attaching a note to the manuscript. You might add that although the work makes a contribution to knowledge, in places the drift of the argument is unclear; in some chapters simple introductory passages are needed to orient the reader; in others the presentation could be streamlined (or expanded) in the interests of clarity; and so forth. Send examples or mark the places in the manuscript.

The author is delighted that you find the work admirable, although distressed that flaws were found as well. The author becomes a victim of mixed emotions, unable to condemn you completely, so the positive confidence may crack a little and suggestions be considered, for you have reaffirmed what the author knows and feels: the work is good! This author may then concede that you might possibly also be right in asking for changes.

THE ROLE OF APPRECIATION

I believe it is sometimes a waste of effort for a copyeditor to try for bright or original remarks in such exchanges. Standard forms, even clichés, are often appropriate: "We are very happy to be publishing your work" makes an author happy. Or write: "Please do not hesitate to get in touch with us by e-mail, phone, fax, or letter if you have any questions." Such gracious formalities are useful, and expected, in the relationship.

Editors could express appreciation of their authors more often. Stylebooks may give all the precepts on style and usage that an editor needs, but a little appreciative comment may be the editor's ally in regularizing spellings, enforcing rules of punctuation, and generally improving a writer's style.

The time spent in identifying and mentioning the good in a piece brings two benefits: the likelihood of better relations with the author and the hope that when editors approach a manuscript looking for the good in it they will be able to enhance that good with editing.

FIVE

Editorial Procedures

Many publishers do the preliminary checking on manuscripts in-house and then send them to freelancers for copyediting; others use in-house editors at various stages. Rarely does one editor procure, evaluate, and copyedit.

BASICS

But whatever the assignment of responsibilities, after the decision to publish has been made, certain attentions are given to all manuscripts: checking, cross-checking, counting, consulting (dictionaries, encyclopedias, atlases, manuals, guides, other editors, other authors), and thinking, puzzling, deciding, and making every jot correct, consistent, concise, and clear.

Choices

Editorial procedures for computer-generated book composition differ from those used in preparing manuscripts for traditional typesetting, although of course the aim of copyeditors in both instances is the same.

So it is possible to discuss the goals of all copyediting precisely, while the hands-on moves made by copyeditors in different publishing houses may vary widely, depending on what electronic coding is favored, which brand of equipment is being used, or whether typescript has to be dealt with.

Since most authors now create manuscripts electronically and submit both disks (or diskettes, if you please) and hard copy to a publisher, a choice is presented as to the method of editing. It may be done onscreen or on the printout. Onscreen is preferred in most houses, but some editing is still done on paper. Whatever, the editor digs in and reads through, applying all the old-fashioned and new-fashioned rules of grammar and composition to ensure that the text is correct, concise, clear, and consistent.

Generic Coding

Along with routine copyediting, the editor's concurrent task is to code headings, footnotes, indentation, diacritical marks, and any special type. The editor working onscreen may also code for design if that has already been decided. The generic coding used is not specific as to computer or program; each publisher has a preferred code, and there are many. Angle brackets may be used to enclose coded directions about what is to appear. Comments and questions for the author may be placed within brackets or braces or exclamation points or printed as footnotes. Other systems use shading or lines to indicate deletions. Additions may be underlined, shaded, or in color. But despite this variation in details what is going on is obvious, and the editor has specific directions on how to proceed. The coding of course is signaled to disappear before printing.

Instructions for electronic copyediting stress the following cautions: (1) Take care that your suggested deletions, however indicated, are still legible. (2) Make sure that the author understands and will accept, reject, or revise your editing while saving all suggestions. (3) The final corrections you will make onscreen yourself later, but the course of revisions is saved in a printed document and on disk as a matter of record.

Here are a few samples from one of the many generic codes: <cn>

chapter number; <ct> chapter title; <cot> chapter opening text; <bt> body text; <ext> extract; <bq> block quote; <i> italics; <h1> number 1 subhead; <a> acute accent. End codes can be signaled generically by </> or keyed to the code you wish to exit (for example, </i> end italics), but they are rarely used since a new code indicates the end of a code.

PRELIMINARIES

When a manuscript (most likely a disk, with hard copy) is turned over to you as copyeditor, this may be the first time you have seen the work. Thus begins a process that will end when the edited disk or typescript is passed on to the compositor or printer for manufacturing into a book.

Before starting, however, you should see to it that a small library of aids is available, some directly at hand, others in the vicinity—at hand an unabridged dictionary, a concise dictionary of recent date, and one or two manuals of style and usage; nearby special reference books suited to the project under way. (The "Annotated Bibliography" at the end of this book will assist editors in choosing what is essential, what may help, and what it would be nice to have.) For help with checking manuscripts, some editors are turning also to the vast assortment of facts available online—the contents of dictionaries, thesauruses, encyclopedias, and so forth. Internet reference sources are a considerable convenience.

The first step in the editing process is to make sure that all the manuscript is at hand or accounted for. Any missing parts, perhaps a map or a chart or acknowledgments, may be—should be—referred to in the information about the manuscript provided by the editor handling it earlier. With automatically numbered computer copy you will have to trust the author that no pages are missing. With typescript or hard copy, make sure, by counting the pages, that none have been inadvertently omitted or included twice.

Chapter Titles and Headings

Next get a bird's-eye view of the manuscript and form a notion of what this book-to-be is about. Check chapter titles and chapter numbers, part titles and numbers if any, and subheads if any as given in the text against the titles and numbers listed in the table of contents in the front matter (the opening pages before page 1 of Chapter 1). If the headings don't match exactly, query the author about any discrepancies or make the preferable choice when it is obvious. When dealing with hard copy or a typed MS, a sheet of colored paper slipped between chapters will make it easier to find your way around in the manuscript.

Headings may fall into several orders: main heads, subheads, sub-subheads, and so on. The editor working onscreen marks the chapter heads and subheads according to the publisher's generic code. The editor working on typescript marks each heading of a given order in the margin with a numeral or letter (circled); for example, all chapter titles might be marked A, all subheads 1, all sub-subheads 2. Italics in chapter titles or subheads or heads running consecutively should always be noted on a style sheet for the designer.

Now is the time for a preliminary examination of the chapter titles and subheads. Do they make sense and seem to be helpful indicators of the plan of the book? Are they parallel in construction and consistent, not here a sentence, there a prepositional phrase, elsewhere a noun or an adjective? Also keep in mind that subheads are not part of the text grammatically; the thought should be complete without them. Thus under a subhead "Chickens" the first sentence should not start, "These birds. . . ." Sometimes every or almost every chapter title begins with "The." Can, or should, something be done about this, for appearance's sake? You will need to keep these questions in mind for answers that may come during the editing.

Illustrative Material

Illustrations can be referred to in the text most readily when they are numbered, preferably by chapter. The author should have provided legends, or captions, for each. If there are to be lists of illustrations in the front matter, check these against the legends and against the artwork or tabular material in the text.

Handle photographs and other illustrative materials carefully. Illustrations should be numbered on the back and identified with the author's name. If there are many, they can be numbered by chapter, as 1.1, 1.2, and so on. But do not write with a sharp pencil anywhere on photographs, and use only the margins or the back for directions; also be careful not to smudge photos with fingerprints. Do not use tape or paper clips on photographs or artwork.

The text should not refer to "the figure above" or "the figure below" since in making up the pages a specific figure may not fall "above" or "below." Simply refer to it by number. Customarily figures follow mention in the text.

Later make sure that the style of labeling is consistent throughout, that elements referred to in the text correspond with the same elements in the illustration. At this point it may be easier to change the text than the illustration. Note on the back of the illustration the page of the text it should accompany and mark in the text about where the illustration preferably could go: "Fig. 2 about here," shaded on disk (or whatever), circled in typescript. (These directions are designed to assist the printer when the edited illustrative materials along with the edited disk or typescript are passed on from the production department.)

At this point in the editing you already know something about the author. If everything matches perfectly or nearly so, it's an unusual author. If only a few discrepancies show up, it's an average, not-bad author. If many inconsistencies are evident, it's an erratic author who must be watched every step of the way, someone who may well be a brilliant writer but who lacks the eye for details that you as copyeditor, fortunately, bring to the task.

Notes and Bibliography or References

When there are footnotes (or endnotes), check the numbering in the text and on the notes by counting in both places and confirming that the last numbers agree. Note numbers in the text of computer-generated copy or in typescript need to be coded or marked for superscripts, which are small numerals or letters above the line. (For an explanation and illustration of editing changes, see figures 1 and 2 in the Appendix.) If a note is added or deleted after the initial numbering, all notes following *must* be renumbered.

Check the alphabetization of the bibliography or references. The preferred system of alphabetization to determine the order of entries is letter by letter, as in *participles, parts of speech, part titles*. Also acceptable is a system of order determined word by word, as in *part titles, participles, parts of speech*. The system chosen of course must be used consistently. (More details are given under "Alphabetization" in Chapter 9, "Notes, References, and Bibliography.")

You will read the notes and bibliography later and will then judge whether the form, or style, is suitable and used consistently.

In some publishing houses the preliminary operations are done by an editorial assistant and so may be noted on a checklist for copyeditors. (A sample checklist is given at the end of this chapter.)

All this checking, though routine, will be interesting and productive if you keep in mind that a *book* is taking shape and that your editing is contributing to the elegant contours of the finished product.

Front Matter

Turning to the front matter, you first add a false title page—giving only the main title (and series title if the book is in a series)—to precede the title page. Following the title page comes the copyright page, which includes the book's Library of Congress Cataloging-in-Publication Data and International Standard Book Number (ISBN). It should also contain any special conditions of copyright supplied to you by the acquiring editor.

Front matter also may include some or all of the following: a dedication, epigraph, table of contents (called "Contents"), list of illustrations (called "Illustrations") or figures or charts or tables, foreword (not by the author), preface and acknowledgments (by the author), and a half title (just the title). All these precede page 1 of the text, which you should code or mark as such. For a valuable assist, lay hands on copies of similar books issued by your publisher to use as models of format.

You can start the long haul by reading the front matter and making notes on possible problems. It is not necessary at this point to spend much time on the preface or introduction; these you will carefully edit afterward. For the present you are merely finding out what the author is attempting to do in this book.

Pages of front matter in the manuscript often appear as lowercase roman numerals in the book. (Numbering front matter separately sets it off from the main text and makes possible adding or subtracting a page or two at the final stages of production, when deleting an expendable page may save having a number of blank pages at the end of the book.)

COPYEDITING

Now you are ready to dig in on page 1 of the text. The number of possible changes that you as editor could suggest is almost infinite. But you must remember what you are there to do.

Errors, Ambiguities, Inconsistencies

First, you are primarily looking for lapses: mistakes in spelling or grammar, syntax or construction, while keeping an eye out for errors of fact and, more difficult to detect, unsound reasoning or faulty analysis. Second, you endeavor to spot any wording that is unclear or ambiguous. If two or more different meanings could be read into a passage, the author may have to decide which is right. Third, eliminate inconsistencies: in spelling (catalog/catalogue), in terminology (World War II/Second World War), and in format, especially in footnotes and bibliography. Any publisher can be blamed, and sometimes is blamed in reviews, when errors or inconsistencies show up in books.

Style of Writing

Last, you may help with style of writing, although how much help may be determined by the publisher's sense of the importance of the book, the amount of editorial time and press time to be invested in the book, and finally the willingness of the author to accept suggestions. Here is where infinite possibilities become finite. You may have to forgo suggesting niceties of expression except for the unusual book and the unusual author. Clarity is an essential component, felicitous expression a grace note. As a copyeditor though, I make a few standard stylistic changes. In place of the all-purpose word "things," for example, I always try to substitute a more precise term, such as "ideas," or "facts," or "characteristics," or "hopes and fears," or "baseball bats and gloves." Deleting *very* will usually strengthen rather than weaken a statement, and changing some passive verbs to active is easy to do and worth the effort.

In writing, we should value conciseness. William Strunk's command in *The Elements of Style* should be the standing order of every editing day: "Omit needless words!" Those who obey this command will win the war of words, save on production costs, and achieve a worthy economy of expression. Deleting a superfluous word or two, the simplest kind of editing, brings great rewards: in "No useful purpose is served," delete *useful*; in "He raised his arm up," delete *up*. When four words are used instead of five, efficiency and style are improved by 20 percent.

In sum, copyeditors want every piece of writing under their hands to be correct, clear, consistent, and concise. Anything less wastes everybody's time. How close can they come to this goal? Pretty close—using tact, perseverance, and skill.

Certain props make this exacting job easier. In addition to dictionaries and style manuals, you may need a biographical dictionary, a gazetteer or atlas, foreign-language dictionaries, encyclopedias, and other compendiums of facts. Right at hand, if you have the capability, is the Internet array of information aids, now a boon to editors. But a shelf of reference books is still a handy standby. Of course you may ask authors themselves to check names, dates, and other facts, but often a quick look into a reference source to settle a question will save time.

STYLE SHEET

An essential tool is the style sheet you prepare as editing proceeds. For computer users, some software programs provide style-sheet capability. With hard copy or typescript take a large sheet of paper, preferably in a distinctive color for easy locating, rule it off into three columns headed, say, A–J, K–S, T–Z, and note on it as they come up all words, roughly alphabetized, that have alternative spellings (*envelope/envelop*; *theater/theatre*). Include the page number of the first occurrence and maybe subsequent page numbers if there is any chance of switching to an alternative form. Also record on the style sheet the use of capital letters, italics, and hyphens, problem areas where dictionaries differ and usage varies. Consistency is the goal. Some manuscripts may require a separate style sheet just for names and titles.

This rough style sheet is for the editor's convenience, not to be confused with the finalized style sheet that is passed along with the edited text for use by the author and the press.

Capital Letters

Briefly, some capitals are determined by the facts: the name of something is capitalized. Many other capitals may depend on house style, the author's wishes, or usage in the field of study (federal, classical, gestalt, impressionism—these can go either way). No set rules pertain except that the complete proper name of something is capped (Cornell University), although subsequent short references may be lowercased (the university) or remain capped. The guiding principle is to decide and be consistent.

Italics

In brief, considerable latitude in italicization is acceptable. While dictionaries differ (as on *mañana* and *ancien régime*), the trend is toward roman type (ad hoc, ibid., ipso facto). But the author and editor may wish to retain italics for such terms as *ad hominem, ciao,* or *joie de vivre.*

Hyphens

Hyphens are a special problem, for the ongoing trend is to forgo them, and the unabridged dictionaries may be behind the times. For new words and recent combinations, an editor may wish to refer to a concise dictionary of most recent date, but disagreements persist there too. Check the latest *Webster's Collegiate* (1993, 1999) and the *Illustrated Oxford* (1998), and you will find the following: *mind-set* and *mindset*; *heartrending* and *heart-rending*. It helps to know which dictionary the author has used. (Chapter 7, "A Concise Manual of Writing Style," gives full details under "Capitalization," "Italics," and "Compound Words and Hyphens." See also "Computer Language" in Chapter 6, "Computer Technology.")

Copyeditor and *copyediting* have a curious history. *Random House* is my authority for using the one-word form. But *Webster's* agrees with *Oxford* on *copy editor*, although *Webster's* favors *copyedit* as a verb. They both sanction *copyreader* and *copywriter*, with verbs to match. The *Webster's* definition for *copyreader* is *copy editor*. I have reasons for my choice, and so do the lexicographers; copyeditor, assume an author has reasons too, and don't spend time adding or eliminating hyphens except to achieve consistency. If the author is inconsistent, you may need to confer. (Incidentally, all three dictionaries agree on *freelance* and *freelancer*.)

When a hyphenated word breaks after a hyphen at the end of a line on typescript copy, double the hyphen (=) to direct the printer to retain it. Some copyeditors further indicate "close up" for hyphens at the end of a line that are not to stand, particularly when there is a possibility of ambiguity. The editor also needs to code or mark hyphens that should be set as en dashes (pre–Civil War).

SPECIAL PROBLEMS

Signal unusual format (poetry, parallel columns, special type, diacriticals) or possible problems in design (lists, outsize tables, two levels of headings running consecutively). Call attention to Arabic, Greek, Hebrew, Hindi, and other foreign alphabets, as well as to mathematical and chemical symbols; the pound sterling (£), the yen (¥), and other moneys; sharps and flats; indeed any symbol. Various codes are available for all these. Mark extracts (block quotations and poetry) so they can be set however the designer decides. On old-fashioned typescript use a line in the margin close to the text and write "extract" or "poetry," circled.

CORRECTIONS

In making corrections the copyeditor aims to keep the manuscript neat and legible and to retain as much of the author's keyboarding as possible, to keep the changes unobtrusive, rather than trying to show how bad the manuscript was and how much has been done to improve it.

In phrasing questions for the author, try to be brief and direct the author's attention to altering the text, not to answering questions. On disk, use the provided instructions for coding queries: for example, one system requires that you append brief comments and queries as asterisk notes. On paper, you can use the margins for short questions, but attach colored (preferably old-style gummed) stickers to provide space for longer queries and remarks or write "pto" (please turn over the page) in the margin and the query on the back of the page.

One effective scheme for requesting changes is to use symbols for recurring problems, such as a check where a passive verb could be changed to active or an asterisk where a word or phrase is overused. Particularly useful with an author addicted to overuse of adverbs or adjectives is the device of marking an X where these qualifiers get in the way. But I should temper advice about adverbs with a caution. One author used *obviously, clearly,* and *certainly* so many times that in the end we both were embarrassed. At first he thanked me kindly for pointing out the repetition: "Bravo!" "Touché!" he wrote in the margin beside the Xs of the early chapters. But when his discomfiture (obviously) turned to distress over the profusion of Xs, he lashed out at me from the manuscript: "Why do you hate these words so?" The Xs (clearly) had generated more than just a spirit of cooperation. While calling attention to flaws in a manuscript, you may indeed arouse emotions that interfere with progress. Well, I might say, nothing ventured, nothing gained (certainly).

Yet a kindlier method would be to make the deletions yourself and say, "I've deleted some words that seem overused, hoping you agree. If not, restore as you wish."

Figure 1 in the Appendix shows sample pages to illustrate how coded changes look on a computer printout; Figure 2 shows changes made on typescript. These pages are not typical because they are overloaded with corrections.

FINISHING UP

When the manuscript was handed over to you, a packet of materials came with it, including perhaps an estimate of production costs, an acquisition editor's comments and correspondence, and, most important for you, one or more reader's reports. Along the way you will have noticed whether or not, or how well or not, the author took care of all the readers' suggestions. Perhaps one more approach to the author by you will accomplish the suggested improvements, assuming you are not obliged or do not want to discuss the problem with the acquiring editor first.

Running Heads

Copy for running heads (headings at the top of each page) has to be prepared and included with the manuscript. The designer may be the one to decide which type of running head will suit the book. One choice is to place the book title on the left and on the right the chapter title, perhaps shortened to fit the width of the page by using the first part or the most descriptive part of the title, somewhat as follows:

Chapter Title	*Shortened Running Head*
Textual Notes on the *Clouds* of Aristophanes	Textual Notes on the *Clouds*
Government, Society, and Culture in al-Andalus, 711–1031	Government, Society, and Culture in al-Andalus

| The Latin Poems of Giovanni | The Latin Poems of Pico |
| Pico della Mirandola | |

Other, currently often preferred, options show the chapter title on both sides or the chapter number (Chapter Ten) on the left and the chapter title (A Song for Mr. Biswas) on the right. Or, if the book has a tag under the chapter title, use the title on the verso (Slavery) and on the recto the tag (Our Past Is Never Far Away). When a book has parts, a part title can go on the left or, with a multiauthor collection, the authors' names on one side and the article titles on the other.

When notes are placed at the back of the book, special running heads are sometimes provided to assist the reader, perhaps the chapter number and short title, as "2. The Latin Poems of Pico."

Spine Copy

Lettering to be imprinted on the spine of the book's binding includes the author's name (last or full), the title of the book (often without the subtitle), and the imprint of the publisher. Some houses ask the editor to supply this copy and to check proof of it.

Review

After handling the text, notes, and bibliography or references, you should return to the front matter and now, with full knowledge of what the book is about, judge whether the introductory parts are adequate. Does the author keep the promises made? Is the preliminary overview accurate? You must test the author's forecast and, if it is found wanting, edit it. Strong, clear, suitable introductory pages can provide salespeople with a pitch, reviewers with quotes, and readers with expectations that will be realized.

As a safeguard that editors take all necessary steps in processing manuscripts, some editorial offices customarily have a detailed checklist for editors. If so, review it to make sure that everything has been taken care of.

Sample Checklist for Copyeditors

Title of book (including subtitle) _____

Author's name _____

Date received for editing _____

Parts missing _____

_____ 1. Pages counted.

_____ 2. Files checked again for relevant information, including readers' reports and author's responses as to whether something was *done* or *not done* about readers' suggestions.

_____ 3. Contents page checked against part titles, chapter titles, subheads, and numbers. Lists of tables, charts, and illustrations also checked.

_____ 4. Heads and subheads marked [often done during editing].

_____ 5. Chapter ends marked [can be done while editing].

_____ 6. Notes and note numbers checked.

_____ 7. Extracts (long quotations) styled [usually done while editing].

_____ 8. Legends (headings) provided for figures, charts, illustrations, etc.

_____ 9. Numbering of tables, figures, charts, illustrations, etc., corresponds in front matter, in text, on legends and artwork.

_____10. Placement of tables, figures, charts, illustrations, etc., indicated [usually done during editing].

_____ 11. Alphabetization of bibliography/references checked.

_____ 12. Permissions already taken care of by an editor or, if not, signaled as yet to be done.

_____ 13. Front matter complete.

_____ a. Preface or acknowledgments signed with author's name or initials [if the publisher wishes].

_____ b. Copy for running heads provided.

_____ c. Spine copy provided if needed from editor.

_____ 14. Design problems, unusual diacritical marks, and foreign alphabets noted for production.

_____ 15. List of codes used [to aid the designer and typesetter].

_____ 16. A style sheet [if necessary].

EDITOR TO AUTHOR

At this point a printout (hard copy) from the disk (or disks) the editor has been working on—or the edited typescript—is sent to the author. Along with this mailing should go standard instructions:

1. Please do not obliterate queries, for the editor will need them when reviewing the manuscript.

2. Call attention clearly to any changes or additions you make, using a colored pen or pencil (red is good).

3. Check all quotations, foreign words, names, and references for accuracy.

It won't hurt to add something about how much you enjoyed working on the manuscript and maybe something about the publisher's hopes for the book, because the author may be appalled by how much there is yet to do. You may know that this is an average manuscript with a normal amount of editorial problems, but it probably won't seem so to the author. The number of changes and queries may seem excessive until the author has dug in and started dealing with each one. Ask the author, as graciously as possible, to consider the suggestions one by one and adjust the text in response to the queries. If the author regenerates pages from the computer, or rewrites, and thus creates new copy, the old manuscript should also be returned, so the editor can see that corrections were not lost. You must stress that after the review the manuscript should be in its final form, ready for the printer. No further changes may be made without incurring charges for author's alterations.

Some publishers do not permit a freelance editor or a copyeditor to be in touch directly with the author. A house editor then must keep in mind these considerations and communicate with the author. But whoever does it, the author needs to be reassured of retaining control over the book while cooperating with the staff at the press. This gentle urging, paired with true appreciation, is now just as important as all the work already done. You must win the author over if a better book is to be achieved. Being careful and accurate is not enough; being accepted as a helper and well-wisher completes your assignment.

SIX

Computer Technology

The computer has revolutionized publishing, as it has changed much else in the marketplace. But the prime mover in the publishing business, the author, may not have changed much, yet. Indeed, an informal poll I took among managing editors revealed an opinion common to those who should know. The question was: "Would you say that computer technology, which facilitates making changes (presumably improvements) on manuscripts, has resulted in a better quality of writing?" The answer was direct and simple: "No—the manuscripts are longer, since it's easier to produce designer copy. Authors are writing more but not better."

We editors should say, "Thank goodness! We'll still have our jobs."

But hold on. Our authors have mastered the techniques of computer use. Perhaps we shouldn't worry that their writing is wanting or mimics the style of current software packages. A bright future may offer other options. Maybe the electronic industry with its analysts and synergists will develop customized software packages enabling authors to command the style of established writers—say, Thomas Hardy or Carl Sagan or Justice Frankfurter. Ordinary people may become more distinguished writers. And editors, intermediaries between the author's computer and the publishing house, will surely still be able to assist in making better books.

THE PUBLISHING HOUSE

Most publishers use computer files in the publishing process (although they may also request hard copy for submission and editing purposes). Yet manuscripts arrive as well on enhanced-capacity zip disks or on CD-ROMs, or often by e-mail. Editing procedures vary, depending on the publisher's equipment and customs and the publishing house's capability of transforming whatever comes in to its preferred system. If disks are submitted, the first step is to convert them, if necessary, for use on the publisher's equipment.

The publisher's individual generic code then provides the means by which the editors at that house exercise their computer skills. An international standard for generic tagging, Standard Generalized Markup Language (SGML), is making headway, but as yet the multiplicity of codes persists. They work.

For the manuscript that comes to the publisher as typed copy, technology has also provided a means called scanning for transferring this text into a computer file. When a publisher wishes to handle every manuscript in the same format, the manuscript not prepared on a computer is scanned before copyediting. Scanners, however, may introduce mistakes, and an editor working on such a manuscript must watch for this new breed of error (for example, commas rendered as periods, or a word such as *burn* given as *bum*). Publishers also use keyboarding services, which usually employ two people to type in the material provided on hard copy. Errors are detected by comparing the two new versions, and the resulting final file is more than 99 percent accurate.

COMPUTER AIDS

Much help in editing comes from the computer's built-in systems, but the editor needs much skill to access these aids. Primarily we can think of the computer as a super typewriter that comes equipped not only with a fantastic memory and considerable knowledge but also with a super eraser, an electronic scissors for cutting and pasting, tags that don't fall off, and a pica ruler that automatically counts lines and spaces.

Indexes and cross-references can be kept in the computer database. The computer can search the entire document for a particular word or phrase and note the pages where it is found. This search can also be used to replace a particular word with another word in all or just some occurrences. Tables can be converted and edited onscreen. Charts, graphs, and artwork can be supplied on disk or as camera-ready copy and added to the typesetter's files. Available also is a vast repository of information for checking facts via the Internet.

Software accessories provide extra maneuverability. A spell checker is basic and can be taught new words, but it won't signal an error when *it* appears instead of *is* or *now* instead of *not*, all words correctly spelled. These kinds of mistakes are commonly found in recent publications.

A grammar checker is a built-in dictator without ultimate power: although Microsoft *Word* disapproves of my long sentences and chides me with long green underlinings (including one under this perfectly proper sentence), I can click "Ignore all" to reject these comments. (Oh, how Shakespeare would have suffered from this software's judgments!) So a writer might wish to be wary, lest unwelcome elements in the style of the software package become the style of the book.

Amazingly, though, with the right software, this machine can detect a plural subject with a singular verb. That's genuine assistance.

EDITOR ON COMPUTER

A live person with judgment controls all. Although electronic assists are available, a personal check is still critical, as a computer cannot of course test for sense and/or nonsense ("Purple apples swiftly rob helpful trucks in the new music" does, of course, pass the machine's grammar and spelling checkers).

Spacing between words and after punctuation may need to be corrected. If the computer screen shows no space after a period, space must be added. The editor also must know the publisher's code for unusual characters (Greek and other foreign alphabets, mathematical and chemical symbols, money, sharps and flats, and all the rest).

The editor sends the author printouts of the work at various stages of production: first, hard copy containing the editing (the "redlined" version); next, hard copy showing the author's final changes and responses to editing as keyboarded in (equivalent to galley proof); and, finally, page proof. (The procedures are further explained in Chapter 5, "Editorial Procedures," especially under "Generic Coding," and in the opening pages of Chapter 11, "Proofs and Index.")

The editor working on disk also has to follow computer backup and virus control procedures: first, label the original manuscript disk and the printout, and keep them in a secure location; then ensure that a procedure for tracking future edits and changes is in place. The record of manuscript changes usually consists of labeled printouts and disks. These are useful in the event of technical troubles, accidental deletion, or other gremlins. Computers perform with great speed; pages, sections, chapters can be zapped accidentally with similar dispatch.

AUTHOR ON COMPUTER

Editors should offer authors instructions and cautionary words:

The type font chosen should be large enough for an easy read and have clear, well-formed letters (no descenders that could be blocked out by underlining, or *V*s that look like *U*s, or ones that look like els, or commas that look like periods).

General directions about publishers' preferences are especially helpful: for example, to begin each chapter in a new file; to name each file clearly indicating its contents; not to use fancy display fonts for headings; to keep formatting to a minimum; and to place tables, charts, and graphs in separate files. Since publishers have important requirements for and advice about using computers to produce manuscripts, editors should get these recommendations to authors as early as possible.

After acceptance of the manuscript, the author, in addition to supplying both a disk and one or two printouts, doubtless will be asked to guarantee that disk and printout match. The author of course should be warned to keep a printout, as well as backup copies of the disk(s).

The same contractual agreements customarily exist between author and publisher as with a hard-copy manuscript. The manuscript of a book in progress—be it computer printouts, or disks, or e-mail attachments, or typed pages—is a valuable document, a record of changes. The author needs it to verify that changes made by the copy-editor are correct and appropriate; the editor needs it to check what the author has done; the publisher needs it as a record of who did what. The computer user needs it as a safeguard against erasing material on a disk accidentally or having a paragraph appear in the book twice because it was not deleted from spot A when it was moved to spot B.

COMPUTER LANGUAGE

During late-twentieth-century decades new meanings for hundreds of words showed up to describe the new objects and operations associated with the computer. A *mouse* (with electronic DNA) is the chief operator, moved about on a *mousepad* to give *commands*. It asks the machine to *save* or *print* what has been keyboarded and stored in a *file*. With a *click* or *double-click*, it can order the machine to *copy, cut, paste, delete,* and perform other tasks. An *icon* is a picture onscreen representing a program, a file, or other item; a *menu* is a list of commands appearing onscreen; a *window* is a rectangular portion of the screen that displays an open program or the contents of a folder or disk. (See also "New Uses for Old Words" in Chapter 8, "The Fine Art.")

While computers are becoming more efficient and user-friendly, computer language is changing as fast as the machinery. A few years ago *diskette* seemed to be the preferred term for the 3.5-inch round plate we all are now using (and some diehards continued to use the old *floppy disk* and *floppy*). But many twenty-first-century writers are using the shorter form *disk*. Editors will have to keep alert and perhaps be tolerant toward the author who hasn't read the latest online handbook—or toward one who has. I join the herd favoring the simpler term. No reason except current usage, that powerful determinant.

Similarly, *e-mail* (with the hyphen) appears in print to be the voters' choice in 2002, but *email* is probably just around the corner.

RESULTS

As the publishing industry luxuriates in the ease and speed, the useful complexity, and the continuing improvements provided by computer technology, authors too are enjoying its benefits. Most important for authors is the ready availability of clean copy. And the spell checker, grammar checker, and other options all make manuscript preparation easier.

Editors are favored with similar ease in making changes, but the editor now has the added responsibility of coding the manuscript for format and sometimes design. Yet the editor thus can become more closely involved in the task of bookmaking. The use of disks requires close cooperation between editorial and production departments. In some houses the departments have merged. Computer technology also creates even more need for author and editor to communicate and cooperate, and ever more ease in doing so.

Computer processing dramatically speeds up the production of proof, so time, thus money, is saved. Proofreading of type set by a computer is generally faster and easier, since typos are less likely to occur. But occasionally material is dropped, or miscoding causes odd configurations. Proofreading cannot be eliminated, although some in the business suggest it could be skipped.

After printing, the disks will be returned to the publisher for possible future use. For archival purposes disks take up less space than manuscripts. Compositors normally store final book files and film, so minor changes for a reprint can be easily made. In preparing a new edition of a book, the old book's pages can be scanned so the author's changes and new material can then be keyboarded. Sometimes authors make changes directly on tearsheets of the earlier edition, which are then scanned.

So here we are, programmed for the twenty-first century and booted up to go.

While contemplating, in this privileged part of the world, the advantages that our computers bring us, the mind travels to the opposite pole. For computers one needs resources. So this electronic marvel tends to discriminate against the underprivileged. It does not encourage third-world authors and older writers, the Underwood-typewriter authors, unless famous, the young Naipauls of the world. And it does impose incompatible standards on the nonstandardized part of the planet, on the nonstandardized individual. Is this turn of events important? Will it make a difference? Will the publishing business take note of it?

SEVEN

A Concise Manual of Writing Style
for Copyeditors

Editors need not be gifted writers. Some good copyeditors are, some are not. But every editor can profit professionally by knowing a few guidelines that can point a writer in the right direction, toward turning out good prose. As a copyeditor, you can assist authors by applying these professional yardsticks to the work at hand and by suggesting ways authors can measure up.

GENERAL GUIDELINES

Style, when viewed as the outward manifestation of a person's life or even just the cut of one's clothes, has infinite variations. It can rarely be judged as right or wrong but rather as appropriate or inappropriate, interesting or dull, ordinary or extraordinary, perhaps even as noble or ignoble. So also with style in the use of language. Its infinite variations can be judged in many ways. It also can be guided by many rules: for spelling, punctuation, grammar, and, in the effective use of language, by the principles of rhetoric. So, as in life, the sojourner-writer fares better when abiding by the laws and knowing which laws apply.

Rhetoric

Rhetoric is an old-fashioned term for the study of what is one of humankind's greatest achievements: the effective use of language. Spoken or written, words make a difference. So the principles governing their effective use are worth paying attention to, particularly by those wordsmiths—copyeditors.

"A whole," Aristotle says, "is that which has a beginning, a middle, and an end," a principle that can be applied directly to publishing. A good book has a stated purpose or frame of reference (a beginning), disclosure of the author's findings or story (the middle), and a conclusion or resolution (the end). I'd like to say that there are no exceptions to this rule.

A smart beginning is a great plus but difficult to fashion. It should be clear and preferably engaging—or maybe just straightforward. Better avoid a list of chapter titles, which are already plain to see. ("Problem Prefaces and Introductions" in Chapter 10, "Special Editing Problems," offers more on this subject.)

A book's middle usually takes care of itself, but the end can be troublesome. Occasionally an author is satisfied to stop at the end of the middle or the middle of the end. Sometimes the conclusion is too spare or abrupt. What you as copyeditor can do in any circumstance is, while editing routinely, to keep in mind Aristotle's shape of a whole and to focus the author's attention on revising or adding or shifting parts if necessary to provide the satisfying punch of a proper whole.

Another ancient rhetorical principle deserves to be heard: suit one's discourse to the audience. The ancient orators had an audience. For publishing in modern times this maxim has to be put on hold until a question or two can be asked. Is there an audience? Where is it?

Readership

Many authors have hoped that "the general reading public" would share their enthusiasms and buy the book—often a vain hope. Occasionally a book aimed at a small group of readers may have a wider appeal, may have the potential to become a sleeper. Sometimes even a textbook can become a classic, as did *Games People Play* and *Lonely Crowd*. Generally, though, the likely audience is one particular set of readers.

This readership can be roughly estimated by the author, the executive editors, and marketing personnel; it is the basis for the publisher's decision to publish. Readership should be the specific focus of the writer's efforts. Does the writer seriously expect to reach students in classrooms, teachers involved with the subject, scholars working in the area or a related area, or literate readers everywhere? Hitting several of these targets at once is unlikely. The editor needs to know—and encourage the author to be precise about—what the readership of the book may be. The student needs help all along the way. The specialist may be impatient with long explanations. The general reader may expect a lively presentation or a good story. So while editing try to judge whether the author has successfully suited the discourse to the readership. Little or no extra editing time is required for you to keep this goal in mind and to ask the author to measure up to it.

As a copyeditor, you can make a few assumptions about readers. Most readers are not familiar with Greek or Latin, so English translations for these are welcome, as indeed for any foreign language—even French or Spanish. A majority of readers will appreciate definitions of terms important to the discussion; clarification of technical language is useful, despite the risk of telling some readers what they already know. A phrase to identify people not commonly known will annoy few readers. But introduction of too many characters at once is troublesome, and sometimes a reader needs help to identify a person who has been absent from the story for a while.

When acronyms are used for names of little-known organizations or when obscure persons are mentioned familiarly by last name alone, you should spell out the name of an organization at first mention and supply the first name or initials for each person or ask the author to. You also should supply dates when they are useful or ask the author to. In such matters as these, it is better for the sake of clarity to give rather much information than too little. If perchance general readers take a fancy to the book they will then have the tools for understanding it.

The readership principle has a close relative, whom it assists in action: maintain a consistent point of view. Envisioning a particular group of readers can help a writer hold to one point of view. I myself have struggled with this principle. When I started writing about copyediting, I first published an article titled "A Bag for Editors" and then "A Bag for Authors." In the one I was talking to editors and taking their point of view; in the other I was talking to authors and taking their point of view. When I came to incorporate these articles into a book called *Author and Editor at Work*, I had to revise both articles to take a slightly different point of view, of authors and editors working together: *Making a Better Book*. The present book is beamed at copyeditors. But if authors should care to look over my shoulder at the advice it offers, I'll not complain.

These guidelines show what to aim at; a few others show what to avoid.

Ambiguity

Ambiguity is more than a nuisance. A double entendre is a jolly ploy, but when an unintended meaning comes to mind from a set of words, the writer and reader are in trouble. Another form of ambiguity is subtler: the meaning is not quite discernible; something has been left out; the thought eludes. Do not be shy about noting that you do not understand. The author might well accept that if you don't understand others also might not get the drift. And if an author complains that your editing has altered the meaning, then the author needs to clarify the text.

Repetition

Repetition is often useful, sometimes necessary, at times boring. Be wary when an author writes: "As I have said above," or "as outlined earlier," or "as already mentioned." Perhaps the author does need to refer to information that has been stated earlier, but these half-apologetic asides add nothing and can usually be eliminated without loss. A simple change that works in many cases is to replace the original "as" phrase with "since" or "because" and attach it and what follows to the next sentence. The text reads:

> As mentioned above, chickens tend to run when frightened. When a dog attacked their coop, the birds scattered for half a mile around.

Instead try:

> Since chickens tend to run if frightened, when a dog . . .

Often this maneuver solves the problem. If some such change won't work, rephrase the idea slightly, so it's recognizable but fresh.

Pretentiousness

Pretentiousness and false modesty do show up. Watch prefaces:

> I was fortunate in high school to study under a recognized master of English prose, and my good fortune continued through college, where my mentors were noted authors, whom I wish to thank here.

> My good friend the chancellor of the university has taken much of his valuable time to read my little study and has made invaluable contributions.

Authors who fall into these snares are well-meaning of course, and who would doubt the sincerity of their feelings? You can query: "Isn't this a bit overblown? Better simplify, somewhat as follows":

> I wish to thank my teachers in high school and college, many of whom were themselves accomplished writers.

> Chancellor [so and so] has read the manuscript and offered invaluable suggestions.

And what experienced copyeditor has not faced the following:

> In some places in this book, despite much good advice from friends and colleagues, I have persisted in the error of my ways.

or:

> Although I have had much help in the preparation of this book, I alone am responsible for any errors that may have crept in.

Here you can note: "Of course. Delete?"

These guidelines suggest what copyeditors can hold on to overall while attending to the minutiae of their job. Very little extra time is needed to keep these principles in mind; suggestions to the author on such matters are almost routine, but much can be gained with little effort.

DETAILS

Meanwhile the copyeditor is besieged by details.

Spelling

Every word on every page must be spelled correctly. With spelling, trustworthy assistance is at hand, first in your computer's spell check or for more details in an unabridged dictionary and for quick reference in the collegiate and concise dictionaries. (The "Annotated Bibliography" reviews the dictionaries and will help you to decide which will best suit your needs.)

Here is a list of popularly misspelled words, corrected at the right.

abberration	aberration
accomodate	accommodate
catagory	category
cemetary	cemetery

concensus	consensus
ecstacy	ecstasy
embarass	embarrass
harrass	harass
heighth	height
liason	liaison
remanent	remnant
rhythym	rhythm
strategem	stratagem

Since the national and international celebration of the year 2000, one often misspelled word happily seems to be correctly imprinted in the public memory: *millennium*. But hundreds more remain incorrectly etched. Watch out for -*ible* and -*able*, and -*ancy* and -*ency*. There is no easy rule for suffixes. Consider *pendant* and *dependent*: each in its way refers to a hanger-on. And forget about the old jingle "i before e": *seize* the day. (See also "British Spelling and Punctuation," below.)

Capitalization

The use of capital letters sometimes depends on the facts; proper names are capped.

New York State has a legislature consisting of two houses, the Senate and the Assembly.

In Oregon there is the Legislative Assembly.

Some democratic ideas are to be found in the Republican platform, while Democrats are staunch defenders of the Republic.

Where capitalization can vary depending on the author's preference or usage in the field of study, you must proceed cautiously, retaining forms the author prefers if they work at all well. When an author uses an abundance of caps, you will have to use your judgment in following today's trend toward lowercasing. When an author is inconsistent in capping such terms as *romantic, congressional, court, department,* you can choose lowercase.

Authors sometimes like to capitalize nouns that pertain to their subject (e.g., musicology) or their major interest (i.e., gamelan). Be confident that there is no special justification for such caps, just as there was none when *Time* magazine idiosyncratically capitalized descriptive words (not titles or forms of address) preceding names: Historian Jane Doe, Contractor Joe Dokes, and (get this) Wife Julie.

I use caps for numbered and other parts of a given book, that is, caps for the name of something: Part I, Preface, Introduction, Chapter 1, Figure 1, Table 1, Bibliography, Index. On this practice many stylists agree, but at least one authority recommends lowercase for these parts. Some who opt for caps in the text would accept lowercase abbreviations in reference matter. But always use lowercase *page 1* and *line 1.* (For more on caps see "Differences of Opinion" in Chapter 4, "The Editor's Dilemma," and "Capital Letters" in Chapter 5, "Editorial Procedures.")

Italics

The use of italics is often problematic, for although the trend is toward romanization, dictionaries differ in their recommendations. In the shady areas, follow the author's preference so long as the author does not overuse italics, but choose roman where the author is inconsistent. Many foreign words and phrases, though, are considered part of the English language by lexicographers and hence are no longer italicized. An alert editor will try to curb the tendency of some authors to italicize commonly used foreign words. Restaurant, fiancée, pizza, dachshund, patio, yoga, ego, ski were once foreign words in the U.S. lexicon, and now blitzkrieg, raga, realpolitik, goy, torero, ethos, id, per se, viz., etc., and many others are accepted as English. *Webster's* takes the stance that if the word is in *Webster's* it's English.

A different kind of problem shows up when a foreign word, such as *duende* (Spanish for charm, magnetism), appears continuously throughout a manuscript, say on bullfighting. Since overuse of italic type is distracting, the author may wish to use the foreign term in italics at the first mention only.

Compound Words and Hyphens

For the spelling of compound words and the regulation of hyphens, the latest (now *Merriam-)Webster's Collegiate* and the other abridged dictionaries that are kept up to date are good authorities on current usage. Compound terms are being closed up (copyeditor, checklist) and hyphens are being discarded (colorfast) in the ongoing process of change. Should an author wish to retain a hyphen that has been discarded by the arbiters of fashion (half-way) or to retain a two-word form (good will), you need not quarrel. But watch out that your author doesn't turn modern later on in the text. Here your style sheet helps.

Usage is continuing to eliminate hyphens and apostrophes. Occasionally in this ongoing trend common sense or common clarity requires an inconsistency. Hence we form the plural of *AA* by adding an *s* (*AAs*)—no problem. But a reader might well question what is *aas*, so the plural of *aa* is formed by including an apostrophe (*aa's*). The same goes for *PEs* and *pe's*.

Where there is room for variation—in capitalization, italics, hyphens, and other details—as the copyeditor, in-house or freelance, you may need to consult with the managing or supervisory editor about what kinds of changes to make on the work at hand.

British Spelling and Punctuation

The virtues of British and American usage are often debated. In Britain, single quotes are used initially instead of double and punctuation is placed outside the quotes unless it is already contained in the quotation. *Honour, traveller,* and *programme* are spelled so. *Colour, endeavour, favour, flavour, humour, labour, savoury, vigour,* and so on are favored, as also *labelled, pencilled, soft-pedalled, travelling,* and the like. An *s* is added to *toward* and similar words, and a *c* rather than an *s* in *defense.*

There are also differences in words such as analyze/analyse, dispatch/

despatch, likable/likeable; abridgment/abridgement; combated/combatted, worshiped/worshipped; and dreamt, leapt, learnt, and spelt; woolen/woollen; but skillful/skilful; also meter/metre; draft/draught; plow/plough; not to forget whisky/whiskey. These differences mandated by local custom don't amount to much one way or another, as far as altering or obscuring meaning. But the style of a piece, American or British, must be consistently one or the other and is customarily determined by the place—that is, the country of publication—not the nationality of the author.

A special case shows up with *theater*. Departments of drama now want to be called something like "theatre arts." The spelling *theater* does not set well with many who write about these arts. American dictionaries list *theater* as preferred and *theatre* as acceptable (or in some labeled "Brit."). But since the people in the field, professors of drama, talking about themselves, prefer the *re*, so be it. Editors will get nowhere arguing for consistency: a Theatre Arts Center is not out of the question.

Some American philosophers use single quotes around words used as terms. A logical case of course can be made and is made by British authors to American editors for placing outside the closing quote mark all punctuation that is not part of the quotation. But editors on both sides of the ocean are agents who serve the customs of their place of business, and it is just as easy for an American editor to adjust to British usage as it is for a Londoner, say, to assist a publisher in New York. These exchanges are happening.

GRAMMAR AND USAGE

Parts of Speech

Many writers have favorite parts of speech. Some are fond of adjectives (*interesting, important, necessary, essential, noteworthy,* and the like), especially in the form:

> It is interesting to note that . . .
> It is important to state that . . .

It is necessary to point out that . . .
It is essential to keep in mind that . . .

One of my professors preached that a sentence should never begin with this use of *It is* (or *There is/are*). I believe his dogma was headed aright, though carried too far. But better sentences often can be made other ways. In these instances perhaps the text could show how interesting or essential the point is without declaring it so.

Writers sometimes use adverbs as qualifiers to legitimize inexact statements; too often these remarks are a sign of loose thinking. Expressions such as *for the most part, in essence, basically, fundamentally* encourage often-faulty generalizations.

Adverbs even show up as pseudo substitutes for logic. *Therefore, thus, accordingly, consequently, then* are often used by scholarly writers to provide a framework for a series of non sequiturs. The supposed logical overtones of these words are so strong that many an editor has read serenely through a passage and felt that only by chance did it come through that the *therefore*s and *thus*es were joining disparate elements. Even *moreover*s and *however*s get thrown in helter-skelter. (See also the discussion of adverbs under "Corrections" in Chapter 5, "Editorial Procedures," and the text of Figure 2 in the Appendix.)

Pronouns are a special case. Many writers shy away from them. Instead of *I*, they say *the writer* or worse *this writer*. And if the first person is used, it comes out *we*, for one person (the author), instead of *I*. Truly, *I* is OK. It is a good, sound word, with a specific comprehensible meaning. The opposite fault is using *I* too often.

Prepositional phrases also have many devotees, some of whom pile them up, one after another, with abandon. You may need to revise:

The skill of the author of the first volume of this series of textbooks is considerable. [Grammatically correct but monotonous and wordy.]

Such a sentence could become:

The author of the first volume in this textbook series has considerable skill. [Direct and economical.]

Few writers are unduly fascinated by nouns and verbs, although these parts of speech are the basic elements of communication. Conjunctions, interjections, and articles mostly take care of themselves.

Mistakes in Grammar

Anyone hired as an editor customarily brings to the job a knowledge of the English language and of the grammatical rules governing its use. But any editor confronted by an unedited manuscript understands the need of a good stylebook, such as *The Chicago Manual of Style* or *Copy-Editing: The Cambridge Handbook*. An editor frequently refers to a stylebook, even when she, or he, knows it almost by heart. The authority of a neat typescript at times almost convinces an editor that what he, or she, remembers is wrong. The experienced editor knows when to look in a dictionary or manual. When in doubt, look.

Mistakes tend to recur in manuscripts, and editors might well be alert to catch common slips.

A sentence needs at least a subject and a verb. The subject and verb must agree in number. But notice these mistakes:

Why *does* farmer Brown's chickens cross the road? [Wrong: change to *do*.]

Such mistakes as using the singular verb *does* instead of *do* with the plural subject *chickens* most often slip by when the subject and verb are inverted, as here, or when long complex clauses separate the subject from the verb, or when a singular noun subject is followed by phrases with plural components:

The passel of chickens, turkeys, ducks, and geese *were* eager to see the other side. [Wrong: change to *was*.]

or a plural subject by a singular modifier:

The temperature and moisture in a chicken's environment *is* important. [Wrong: change to *are*.]

Another common grammatical mistake involves the dangling participle:

Struggling to make ends meet, farmer Brown's chickens brought in some extra cash. [Wrong.]

Correcting such an error is not difficult once it has been noticed:

Struggling to make ends meet, farmer Brown raised chickens to bring in some extra cash. [Correct.]

A basic rule, sometimes not heeded, is that pronouns and pronominal adjectives should agree with their antecedents in person, number, gender, and case.

A wise person doesn't count *their* chickens before they're hatched. [Wrong: change *their* to *his* or *her*. Or *A wise person* to *Wise people do not* . . .]

When *he* finds a worm, a hungry hen won't cackle. [Wrong: change *he* to *she*.]

Here again, trouble most often comes when the antecedent is far removed from its referent.

These examples of obvious mistakes are only to warn editors of the kinds of chickens that come home to roost in manuscripts.

Another kind of danger is mixing tenses. In quoting an author long dead, you may regard his writings as living, existing in the present, even though the incidents of his life happened in the past. The choice of tense usually depends on nearby verbs: "Whitman *was* just a clerk in the Attorney General's office, but he *said*, 'I celebrate myself.' " If excerpts are quoted from the poet's work as though from the living present, the present tense can be used: "Whitman *says*: 'Sing on, there in the swamp! / O singer bashful and tender!' "

That and *Which*

Editors and authors quite frequently fall out over the use of *that* and *which* in relative clauses. Some persons tend to use *that* in ordinary speech and *which* when writing; this practice is not sanctioned by the experts. Stylists in the past have ruled that *which* serves best in the nonrestrictive (nondefining) sense, where the clause it introduces is set off by commas, and *that* serves best in the restrictive sense. Many stylists now disregard this time-honored rule. The copyeditor who tries to preserve the distinction is being conservative, and although following the rule might make the author's sentences easier to read and the exposition clearer, if your author thinks the distinction useless and passé and does not wish to observe it, you had better not try. The commas still serve to distinguish between restrictive and nonrestrictive clauses. If frustrated, you might, just here and there, show the value of changing a *which* to *that* and vice versa.

Punctuation

For advice on punctuation, a good manual of style is indispensable. But when an author chooses an optional form, perhaps less preferable than that recommended by stylists, as copyeditor you might well try to avoid arguing (though you may have to if your publisher has guidelines) as long as the author's format is clear. Punctuation is an aid to understanding; the rules have this purpose only.

The comma, the most frequently used mark of punctuation, appears in almost every sentence. You can save time, and possible hassles with an author, by assessing at the start whether the author favors heavy or sparse use of commas. Many writers, following the current trend, omit commas after introductory adverbial clauses or phrases. If the meaning is immediately clear without punctuation no commas are needed. Authors might well be allowed their preference in such instances.

The colon serves many purposes. Properly used it introduces a list, a coordinate clause, a quotation, a question, or an appositive (the last as in, "He recognized only one sport: baseball").

Both dashes and parentheses interrupt the grammatical flow of a sentence. Dashes set apart an aside that is closely related to the thought expressed in the sentence. Parentheses customarily enclose a comment, qualification, or digression and have many other uses in notes and to introduce explanatory material.

And you may have to remind an author that stylists frown on ending a simple declarative sentence with an exclamation point just to express the writer's amazement. (A detailed discussion of punctuation choices is given in Chapter 8, "The Fine Art.")

Abbreviations

Abbreviations in running text are not acceptable to some purists, although such shortcuts as *i.e., e.g.,* and *etc.* are often used in parentheses and certainly in notes. The copyeditor may consider whether these phrases might well be deleted. With *etc.* be sure that enough examples precede to define the *cetera* or that the category is not so exhausted the reader will be hard put to figure out what more items like these could be. *Et cetera* and its variants should be deleted if the listing begins with *such as.*

Cross-References

Internal cross-references to page numbers (e.g., "see p. 00") of course cannot be filled in with the appropriate numbers until page-proof stage, so as a practical consideration they are usually edited out because of the extra expense, possible delay, and the danger of last-minute errors. These changes are counted as AAs and will be charged to the author. An effective device to caution authors about such references is to flag them in the margin with dollar signs ($$). If necessary, cross-references to a chapter or section or to a numbered chart or table can be made instead.

TABLES

Tables in a manuscript will often need your attention. A good table provides information for making a number of comparisons readily. If the categories—column headings and first-column (stub) entries—are well formulated and rightly positioned, comparisons appear at a glance, with data showing ascending, descending, steady, or fluctuating conditions for anything one might analyze: products, population, income, loss, growth, fertility, disease, aptitude, output, skill, years.

Smart editing can improve tables. Logically the stub should have a heading, though often none is given, and many tables pass muster without one. Supplying a head, if only a catchall word such as "Variables," can clarify the categories. If no such term comes to mind, you might query the author but may have to rest with a miscellany of ideas, people, places, times, "things."

Similar tables in a book should be consistent. Watch out for inconsistent usage in column heads (not Physics, Psychiatry, Lawyers) and of course in spelling, hyphenation, and abbreviations.

One category should not have to be repeated again and again throughout a table. Repetition of the percent sign is unnecessary, and better eliminate also any line showing all totals as "100%"—although where such percentages total more, or less, than 100 percent, a note, such as "Rounding off percentages brings the totals to more (or less) than 100%," is needed to account for the discrepancy.

Sometimes you can improve a table by positioning the vertical columns as horizontal lines. This maneuver is useful if the column headings are rather long, since more space is available on the stub.

BIAS-FREE WRITING

One late-twentieth-century social development brought with it the need for special sensitivity in editing. Although current trends in style are toward simplifying, the women's movement for equal rights is causing stylistic complexities: it presents to anyone who uses English a problem (sexist language) that English is not designed to solve. Today a sentence like "A writer should mind his *p*s and *q*s" can make enemies. Some say that at least it should be "*his or her p*s and *q*s*." Others suggest "*her or his p*s and *q*s*." Extremists opt for "*her p*s and *q*s*." *His (or her)* will infuriate feminists; *his/her* will infuriate stylists. An easy out in this instance is to move to the plural: "Writers should mind *their* ps and *qs*."

Some writers of either sex are comfortable with the *he* that stands for human being, but today they risk being labeled on the one hand male chauvinist pigs or on the other traitors to their sex. What should the careful writer or editor (who honors men and women, who cherishes equality for all, and yet may whisper, "Vive la difference"), what should ____ do? No answer will satisfy all parties. There is no good answer, but compromise is possible and necessary.

Copyeditors must be alert to the feminist rejection of customary language and respond. The passive voice also helps in sidestepping the choice of masculine or feminine referents ("*Ps* and *qs* must be kept in mind by a writer"), but this route has to be used cautiously. Both *he* and *she* can be used at critical points, and the sequence altered occasionally. The forms *he, or she,* and *she, or he,* may work well in some sentences; the commas seem to lend equal status, suggesting "as the case may be."

Publishers have issued guidelines to help editors spot offensive stereotyped assumptions—such as expecting secretaries to be women, executives, men. Textbooks have been revised: boys play with dolls, fathers mother babies, girls play with fire engines, and women are mechanics as well as heads of departments. Such awareness is refreshing and causes no trouble with language.

But in general publishers and readers object to a class of so-called sexist terms, and you as editor need to tread cautiously by using inconspicuous variants, some of them new coinages, for the targeted offenders. Avoid a combining form with -*man* if the reference is to a woman or could be to either sex.

Instead of	*Use*
chairman *or* chairwoman	chairperson *or* chair
congressman *or* congresswoman	representative *or* legislator
fireman	firefighter
foreman	supervisor

mailman	letter carrier *or* mail carrier
manhours	workhours
mankind	humankind *or* people
policeman	police officer
salesman	salesperson
spokesman	spokesperson

A caution: you must be careful not to make these alterations when paraphrasing writers who flourished in earlier centuries.

Bias-free language pertains to many topics: gender, sexual orientation, race, ethnicity, religion, disabilities, age. And here "new terms and topics constantly demand recognition, and advice in areas of rapidly changing and hotly contested usage may quickly be superseded" (*Guidelines for Bias-Free Writing*, p. ix). The copyeditor can only try to be aware of and then sensitive to attitudes that may be important to the reading public.

For a last pointer on style, let's look once more into Professor Strunk's "little book," to the "Introductory" of his original *Elements of Style*— a section that does not appear in the Strunk and White editions and is quoted there only in part. Strunk had a large view. He came from the era before there were schools of journalism and courses in creative writing. He thought that any student might well begin by learning to write "plain English." So the professor of literature advised the would-be writer: "After he has learned to write plain English adequate for everyday uses, let him look, for the secrets of style, to the study of the masters of literature" (p. 6). (We hadn't yet progressed to "he or she" or "her or him" in those days.) Either plain English or masterly English. What a sensible choice! Eliminate jargon, gobbledygook, pomposity. Would that we all could.

Editors, as well as authors, need to know good writing when they see it and more particularly to recognize bad writing. Everybody is happy when paragraphs have topic sentences, to smooth the going, and when sections have transitions, to indicate a new direction. Occasionally you can supply a noticeable missing joint, but overall, when time is a consideration, you may have to ask the author to oblige or may just have to skip it (too bad—better make a quick query to the author).

Editors cling to a few good rules. "Omit needless words" is our motto. "Support generalities with particulars" is a good rule. "Have a generality to sum up particulars" can come in handy too.

The details are infinite and time is limited. In today's publishing crunch, pressures to speed up the editing process to save time and money may restrict how much you can do. But let's not bow too low to "progress." With a little practice, you can perform many small tasks at once: correct spelling and grammatical mistakes, smooth the flow of language, fill gaps, query reasoning, ask for checking of facts and even for more information, and encourage authors to hang in there.

When the published book reads well, you and the publisher who employs you are well repaid.

EIGHT

The Fine Art

Copyediting is far from boring. Authors, variegated as they are, help to make it exciting, one way or another. Sometimes their ideas too are exciting, one way or another. Each new author, each new combination of talent and idiosyncrasy, of skill and carelessness, of assurance and timidity, calls for an editor's special appreciation and diffidence.

And rules are changing. Usage becomes standard by use: no king or dictator gives the word; the scouts—Webster, Oxford, Random House, American Heritage, and now Encarta—record what the citizens are doing. Let us hurry then to take note of what is happening now. The scene will change before long. That is part of its charm, the changing scene: new words, disciplines with new languages, computers talking to us, four-letter words in loftier places, old Latinisms in roman type, fewer capital letters, fewer apostrophes, less punctuation. Why, this business is alive!

A copyeditor starting on a manuscript must examine every character in every word of every sentence in every paragraph put forward for publication by this author—a daunting task. You, the editor, in addition to needing an eye for details (the basics), must have an ear for sound prose (the means of communication), as well as a heart to aim for perfection (in the service of someone else). But this predicament is old. Much advice is available.

SENTENCES

Since every piece of prose consists of sentences, variety in the structure of sentences enlivens writing. The form of a sentence also can be adapted to the intended meaning.

A plain simple sentence—just a subject and a predicate—is serviceable and, like a one-two punch, gets the point across straightaway: "Jesus wept" summarizes a long story in two words. With three words the simple sentence can score a knockout: "War is hell." With a slightly more complex predicate, the simple sentence can be forceful and expressive: "He's a grand, ungodly, god-like man." Or add an object for the verb and the simple sentence is powerful: "The soul refuses all limits."

A compound sentence, not necessarily elaborate but with parallel parts balanced, makes comparisons easier in both the telling and the manner of telling: "Cause and effect, means and ends, seed and fruit, cannot be severed; for the effect already blooms in the cause, the end pre-exists in the means, the fruit in the seed." More elaborate compounds, deftly handled, can be enlightening: "Ahab's been in colleges, as well as 'mong the cannibals; been used to deeper wonders than the waves; fixed his fiery lance in mightier, stranger foes than whales." Although we may not hope to write as well as Emerson and Melville, we can at least use their best as models.

A periodic sentence has specific uses. The well-wrought, well-placed periodic sentence pleases everyone—author, editor, and reader. Emphasize "well-wrought," because a periodic sentence is built up, constructed, so that each of its elements, the subordinate clauses and modifying phrases, can be understood as eased into place, but the whole is capped and illumined by the closing words. Smartly designed periodic sentences give distinction, elegance, grace, and sometimes a touch of feeling to ordinary prose. They are especially useful when a writer wishes to call attention to a significant summary or pronouncement:

"The outcast boy and the humble African who find in a union of hearts the strength to defy the angry God of inequality are deathless symbols of the deep current, mightier than the Mississippi, which carries the Republic onward" (from *Are Men Equal?* by Henry Alonzo Myers). This ordering of elements is not a play on words, not a device to embellish prose; it is feeling strikingly expressed and thereby communicated.

William Strunk Jr. and E. B. White and others have something to say about writing periodic sentences. The presumption is that the art of fashioning them can be taught and learned. The average practitioner may not reach emotional heights but can highlight a point effectively. Sometimes an editor, at a critical place in a manuscript, can reorder the parts of a sentence into a purposeful, suspenseful sequence, saving the best till last. Still, this kind of sentence had better not be overused. The suspense and heightened exposition need to be saved for important places.

The most useful sentence of all is the straightforward, informative, declarative statement: "The box was seven feet long, three feet wide, and two feet high." "Verdi was born in the village of Roncole, Italy, on October 10, 1813." Such sentences are the staples of writing. In them the aim is to be clear without question. The danger is overloading. The going gets rough for a reader when too many facts are crammed into one such sentence; then that sentence had better be divided into two or more sentences.

An artful mix of short and long, simple and complex, straightfor-ward and periodic sentences gives prose variety and vigor. A short sentence, among longer, discursive, complex ones, sometimes can bring a picture into focus and imprint it on the memory. A long sentence sometimes can give the composite picture that is needed.

PUNCTUATION

Our written language does not enable us to show the inflections and pauses of spoken discourse. In speech we never say in so many words where periods, commas, colons, and semicolons might come. In read-ing aloud, we leave them out. By means of a pause, a breath, an intonation, we group words in the necessary combinations for communicating thoughts. Since written language does not indicate changes in tone and pauses of speech, these must be shown by the words themselves, by their order and arrangement, and by punctuation. The gifted writer arranges words and punctuation so the rhythm, cadences, and pauses fall naturally and meaningfully.

So, while expressing thought—communication—is the primary function of a sentence, helping to express thoughts is the primary function of punctuation. The rules of punctuation are important guidelines. Sticking close to them enables a writer to cue a reader in quickly to the significance of the words and the order in which they are used. The soundest argument for respecting the rules is that more people are likely to understand the usage and hence will read the message with the least effort: let the reader's attention focus on the thought rather than on the means of expressing the thought. Eccentric punctuation is a hindrance to understanding. It can be used to startle, or to give the reader pause, if that's what's wanted.

But punctuation is both a boon and a nuisance. Along with written words, it enables us to make our thoughts known farther than we can shout. Without it, the words alone might be puzzling to our communicants. Yet the rules of punctuation are a bother, and they are sometimes downgraded by calling them just conventions established by usage. As usage changes, writers are tempted to introduce further changes. This modification, or blurring, of rules of punctuation is ongoing.

How can an editor achieve a satisfactory compromise with old rules? A writer may wish to use as few commas as possible. That's modern and sensible. The old-fashioned rule says that long introductory phrases should be set off by commas. How long is "long"? My rule is: consider whether the reader will at once see where the introductory part ends and the bones of the sentence begin; if the reader cannot be sure, use a comma. In using fewer commas we should not be sloppy but just avoid needless punctuation.

Another old rule is that words out of order in a sentence should be set off by commas. Order in an English declarative sentence has been defined as *subject*, followed by *modifiers of subject*, followed by *predicate*, followed by *modifiers of predicate.* Here too a short out-of-order phrase may be immediately clear without commas. Sometimes the phrase is clear but the commas help in other ways. For example, my comments on punctuation ("Along with written words, it enables us . . ." and "Without it, the words alone . . .") would be clear minus the commas, but since emphasizing the *with* and the *without* is desirable, I used commas. For the sake of nuance a little clutter is added. But the sentences would be considered correct either with or without commas— and the author, not the editor, should decide.

FIGURES OF SPEECH

Metaphors and similes—so-called figures of speech—are as common and as useful in formal writing as they are in everyday speech. They come so naturally to mind that one can hardly avoid them.

New Uses for Old Words

"The *field* of psychology is an important *area* of study." Here are two common, useful metaphors, both pertaining to two-dimensional space and applied to concepts that have no spatial dimension. This *field* is not one of my favorite metaphors, but trying to get rid of it from time to time has given me a decent respect for it. If we speak of *digging into* the field of psychology and *turning up* some helpful insights, we have extended the metaphor and have given it, figuratively, another dimension. General use of these terms in this fashion has added the metaphorical meanings to definitions of the terms. Usage has extended the meanings of countless words, such as *alive, bloom, dribble, drift, horizon, tap, vein, wave.* The language thus is a continuously fertile field for cultivating new metaphorical uses of old words.

Computer usage illustrates this drift today. We have new uses for old words such as *mouse, tower, menu, wallpaper, window, browse, web, icon, hardware, memory.* We have new combines of old words, as *desktop, download, online, e-mail.* And we have new words like *modem,* which is not in the compendious, unabridged 1971 *Oxford English Dictionary*. We can expect more innovations.

When machines started talking to us, a new vocabulary became essential to describe what was being said and how. Early in the twentieth century, the word *print-out* was a less desirable form of *printing-out*, an adjective used to designate photographically sensitized paper. Now *printout* is a noun in computer technology meaning the printed output of a computer. And a new language has evolved.

In this new world, a simple rule is ongoing that changes the syntax of sentences: nouns can be turned into verbs. One can *keyboard* text into a computer. An operator *inputs* data. You *click* on an icon. This development is not new. *Random House* says: "Many verbs in English have derived from nouns. One can *head* an organization or *toe* the mark; *butter* the bread or *bread* the cutlet. Hence, grammatically at least, there is no historical justification for the once frequently heard criticism of *contact* used as a verb meaning 'to communicate with.' *The managing editor contacted each reporter personally.*"

Small conventions have been altered. When I was supervising the editing of a pioneering book on computers, we encountered the word *programming* throughout the manuscript. The author consistently used two *m*s (the preferred British form). The unabridged *Webster* (second edition) gave one *m* as first choice. Our usual practice would have been to follow the dictionary and scratch out all those extra *m*s. A knowledgeable adviser, however, told us that all the people working with computers used two *m*s. So the then unusual spelling was retained. Dictionaries soon began to designate *programmed* and *programming* as "esp. British and Computer Technol." In the 1999 *Merriam-Webster's Collegiate*, *programmed* is listed as preferred.

Metaphors

Extended uses for words and extended metaphors enrich the language. Seldom, however, does one come across a well-worked-out, many-faceted metaphor. "I expand and live in the warm day like corn and melons"—this simple, pleasant simile fits well into a discourse on nature. It could have been expanded and reused, although Emerson does not do so, yet it is in tune with the many metaphors in "Nature." This essay could serve as a manual on metaphors: "Good writing and brilliant discourse," Emerson says, "are perpetual allegories." "In the woods," he says, "I become a transparent eyeball," and his discussion of eyesight and nature stretches the mind. The most satisfying kind of metaphor—like the best of jokes—builds up, develops, expands, and has ramifications.

Sometimes likenesses among disparate ideas are not actually expressed, but terminology from one area of thought is applied to another as never before: "I had better never see a book than to be warped by its attraction clean out of my own orbit, and made a satellite instead of a system." What an illuminating and instructive early formulation of "Trust thyself: every heart vibrates to that iron string"!

The metaphors we admire in poetry may not belong in prose, even in formal, elegant prose. Where is a place for the "still unravish'd bride of quietness," the "foster-child of silence and slow time," save in the ode where they belong? Yet one of the grandest metaphors in the English language is in a prose essay written by the poet Robert Bridges: "If one English poet might be recalled to-day from the dead to continue the work which he left unfinished on earth, . . . the crown of his country's desire would be set on the head of John Keats."

Misuse of metaphors is all too common. Comparisons can be inappropriate or forced or wildly imprecise. The mixed metaphor is the butt of many jokes yet is not easy to avoid. Beware: a rocky road cannot become smooth as silk. A person cannot be soured by constant nitpicking. A crisis cannot spawn a pitfall. An idea cannot be blasted by spiking it or soft-pedaled by sweeping it under the carpet.

Early on as an editor I started to collect mixed metaphors. I had some beauts, many in journals I was editing at the time. I even thought of publishing them. Indeed such examples are amusing—and instructive.

Eventually, though, I decided to throw away my mixed metaphors. For me then the fun was troublesome. If I am to remain in this profession, I thought, I need to be on the side of these muddled authors, and I guess I don't want to laugh, or encourage others to laugh, at their foibles.

Editors are better off, I believe, when they consider themselves on the side of the authors they work with. Now as I am older, and perchance wiser, I still reckon this stance toward authors is appropriate, but I wish I could recall some of those beauts.

NEW WORDS

An editor can never be sure whether or not the author of the manuscript at hand is one of those few who initiate new fashions that later are recorded in dictionaries. If an author wishes to coin a useful word, maybe better be charitable: explain it and use it. Someone had to invent *airdrop* and *moonshot* and *television* and all the useful computer lingo. But judgment and moderation are needed as always. The real issue is what is creativity at work and what is ignorance.

I dislike dividing the world and all the people in it into two oversimplified categories by combining *non* with a noun to form a new word. When such terms as *farmers* and *nonfarmers* or *agriculture* and *nonagriculture* are used, or *music majors* or *nonmusic majors*, the *non* class becomes a nonentity, an amorphous group categorized by not being something. The adjectival forms modifying something, such as *agricultural* and *nonagricultural* products are clear enough, but such terms as *Christian* and *non-Christian*, *white* and *nonwhite*, even *Communist* and *non-Communist*, as nouns or adjectives, by setting one precise specific category against one rough, indeterminate, ill-defined category, can beg the question before the argument begins. If one touch of nature makes the whole world kin, let's not divide the whole world with one little *non*.

CHANGING USAGE

Language constantly changes. Such progress, or regress, soundly documented through generations, appears to be inevitable. So the lexicographer notices these changes being brought into the language by usage. Looking to the future, *thru* just might come into use again, for already it appears on our plastic cards and crosses New York State. But one couldn't recommend that editors let it pass. Similarly, *tho*, an attractive short form, is allowed in dictionaries as "an informal, simplified spelling" but hardly an authorized one.

Some stylists take a superior view of hoi polloi who use *hopefully* in the sense "Hopefully war will not continue in the Middle East." There is nothing for the adverb to modify! Will this usage come into the language? Yes, it already has. The question is: how determinedly will stylists continue to weed it out? The lexicographers who compile our dictionaries, always mindful of usage, are voting with hoi polloi. *Random House* says: "Although some strongly object to its use as a sentence modifier, HOPEFULLY meaning 'it is hoped (that)' has been in use since the 1930's and is fully standard in all varieties of speech and writing: *Hopefully, tensions between the two nations will ease.* This use of HOPEFULLY is parallel to that of *certainly, curiously, frankly, regrettably,* and other sentence modifiers." A strong argument. Dare I predict, hopefully (modifying *predict*), that some good writers will dignify hoi polloi's *hopefully*? As an editor I wouldn't move against it. (For more on *hopefully*, see *The New Fowler's Modern English Usage* under "Stylistic Aids" in the "Annotated Bibliography.")

Then consider *however*. I was taught (yes, it was a long time ago) that *however* should not be used at the beginning of a sentence except in the sense "However difficult conservation is, we must avoid wasting the earth's resources." But don't try foisting this dictum on a philosopher or a sociologist or a logician. You'll find they too often need a form: "However, this line of reasoning is contradicted by recent research." Repositioning the qualifier—"This line of reasoning, however, . . ."—does not alert the reader soon enough to the changed direction of the discourse.

A writer used to be cautioned against using the word *people* in place of *persons* when referring to a number or a group of individuals. The careful stylist used to say, for example, "persons watching the parade" rather than "people watching the parade." The current idiom is moving in the other direction; *people* increasingly is used for the plural *persons*. We would hardly ask: "How many persons are you inviting to your wedding?" We don't customarily say: "Only ten persons showed up for the lecture." *People* still has solid other uses, as in "a people bound by tradition" or "the peoples of South America." Should editors chide writers who use *people* for *persons?* Let us say that the pressure is off, and it may be fruitless to argue or insist.

Years ago, while complaining about mushy thinking, I wrote: Query *perhaps* except in the sense "Perhaps it will rain tomorrow." I objected to statements like: "*Paradise Lost* is perhaps the greatest poem in the English language." I questioned whether the author-authority should be asked to decide: "*Paradise Lost* is the greatest poem . . ." or "one of the greatest poems. . . ." But this mushy *perhaps* shows up so often and is so convenient that prudence and usage suggest an editor had best accept it.

Editors, don't fuss with authors about an *And* at the beginning of a sentence. Writers used to be warned against opening a sentence with a conjunction. But may I add my two cents' worth in support of the judicious use of *And* or *But* or *Yet* or the like at the beginning of a sentence. One of our great, most gifted presidents on official occasions gave us two forthright examples. "*But* in a larger sense," he said, "we cannot dedicate, we cannot consecrate, we cannot hallow, this ground." Later, he summed up straight to the point: "*And* the war came."

Good writers have long been using a preposition at the end of a sentence. So the old proscription against that usage can be dispensed with.

Infinitives are usually better off intact rather than split. Notice, though, that careful stylists sometimes can inject a meaningful adverb into the infinitive form with good effect. A precisely worded "User's Guide" for a computer warns: "Remember to occasionally shift position and move your body." OK.

On another tack, how long can we hold to the distinctions between *affect* and *effect* if common usage is to be followed? Since both terms have valid, different meanings as nouns and verbs, editors can help to preserve these precise variations. Would a miserable sentence such as the following help? "The *affect* that he wanted to *effect* would have *affected* his listeners with adverse *effects.*" A friend says, "This is an affected sentence that is hardly effective."

Note also *comprise*—a neat word when properly used: "The U.S.A. comprises fifty states."

A common use of *either* (meaning each of two) instead of *both* (meaning both of two) is puzzling. "Houses lined *either* side of the road" is acceptable to some editors but in my opinion lacks nicety of expression. Since no one would say "Earrings graced either ear," how do we get to "either side of the road"?

Half a century ago editors observed what seemed like a nicety. One could say: "That is a *worth-while* economy," but, please: "That economy is *worth while.*" At present, editors, the expression is *worthwhile*—no space, no hyphen, as adjective or noun. Usage has consolidated this item. (Further comments on this modernism are to be found under *The New Fowler's Modern English Usage* in "Stylistic Aids" in the "Annotated Bibliography.")

The same fate befell the noun *world view*: first, two words (*Webster's* unabridged 2d ed., 1959, and numerous others in the two decades following); next, hyphenated (*Random House* unabridged 2d ed., 1987); then, one word, *worldview* (*Merriam-Webster's Collegiate*, 10th ed., 1993, 1999), following what the Germans could do in one step with *Weltanschauung*. Perhaps this bit of history will bolster my advice to editors: inform authors of the spelling in your latest dictionary, but don't argue if they are uncomfortable with the latest. Those authors, relying on a recent unabridged dictionary, might be only a few years behind the latest. Or must I argue that, like an atlas of the world, the dictionaries we rely on should be replaced often, say, every ten years or so?

Copyeditors, as arbiters of good taste, have to be judicious yet open-minded, authoritative yet flexible, old-fashioned yet alert with an eye for the tides of change. They then might well dip into the pool of common knowledge, sometimes called wisdom, and fish out an ancient (almost three hundred years ancient), serviceable precept (from Alexander Pope): "Be not the first by whom the new are tried, / Nor yet the last to lay the old aside." Trying to monitor language is not easy and is inevitably frustrating when the tide of usage washes out a favored subtlety. But the language will change, so an editor might well perceive and enjoy the progress, or regress, and the tide.

NINE

Notes, References, and Bibliographies

Reading and editing text can be challenging, enlightening, and enjoyable. Bringing organization and intelligibility to notes, bibliographies, and references is often drudgery. But you do not know your craft if you cannot lay a firm hand on even the most esoteric footnotes.

Yet editing of notes, references, and bibliographies is easier than editing text once you know the possible variations. The general guidelines are clear:

Be consistent.

Be brief.

Abbreviate where appropriate.

If notes and bibliography or references are long and complicated, keep a style sheet (computer-generated or paper) on them. On the sheet, list abbreviations, style of book and journal citations, note format, bibliographical or reference format, and anything unusual.

NUMBERED NOTES

First, before reading the notes, you will have checked and coded or marked the numbering, both in the text and on the notes (as explained under "Notes and Bibliography or References" in Chapter 5, "Editorial Procedures").

Content and Placement

Numbered notes can be placed at the foot of each page, at the end of each chapter, or all together as a section, called endnotes, following the text. When notes appear at the foot of the page, full bibliographical details are customarily given at the first mention in each chapter; if the documentation is meager, however, full details may be given only at first mention in the book. With endnotes that are not complicated, again full details may be needed only at first mention. But with long, complicated endnotes, full details at first mention in each chapter may be helpful. Even at first mention, though, a long form of note can be trimmed down if this kind of editing seems worth the effort:

> 1. Elsie Myers Stainton, *Author and Editor at Work: Making a Better Book* (Toronto, Can.: University of Toronto Press, 1982), pp. 20–21.

> 1. E. M. Stainton, *Author and Editor at Work* (Toronto, 1982), 20–21.

In citing names, the person's preference or the best-known form is often used: Ralph Waldo Emerson, E. B. White. A spelled-out first name or two initials is preferred to one initial only.

The place is customarily given, the publisher optional. The year of publication is informative and is usually included.

Sometimes it is sensible to dissuade an author from using two kinds of notes, such as substantive notes with asterisks as well as numbered references. If the substantive notes are short, they might be incorporated into the text, using parentheses if necessary.

Considerable, almost innumerable, variations are used in notes. One style must be chosen and used with absolute consistency. The editor's job is to ensure this consistency.

Shortening

Here are two extreme examples of note forms, citing a journal; the first is unabridged, while the second shows (1) shortening of author's name, (2) abbreviation of work cited, (3) omission of year when volume number is given, and (4) deletion of issue number when the publication is paged by volume (there are many modifications in between):

> 2. Adam Robert Woolford, "The Adaptability of Gerbils to Light," *Journal of Comparative Psychology*, Vol. XVIII (1990), No. 3 (Sept.), pp. 600–601. [first mention]

> 2. Woolford, A. *J. Comp. Psych.* 18:600–601. [first mention in some disciplines when detailed bibliography is given]

Being careful not to sacrifice clarity, an editor can reduce note length—governed of course by usage in the field. The surname of the author is usually sufficient for subsequent references after the first mention, but if more than one author with a common last name is cited, it may have to be J. Smith or R. Jones. "Vol." is usually omitted, and arabic numerals are preferred to roman numerals, with a space between the journal title and the volume number, no comma. If a journal is paged by volume, the issue number or month can go. Both issue number and month are not needed in many citations but can be helpful. Both volume number and year often are not needed, but again the date may be helpful and is customarily included. For consistency treat a specific journal the same throughout.

PARENTHETICAL REFERENCES

Another form of reference is the parenthetical citation (sometimes called source note) included in the text itself.

(Stainton 1982, 20–21)
(Woolford 1990, 18:600–601)

Note author, no comma, year, comma, pages; and author, no comma, year, comma, volume number, colon, pages.

How much information is given in the reference depends on what is in the text:

Haverstock (1969) wrote the definitive work on the use of green light.

Haverstock thought that the use of green light was dangerous unless skillfully applied (1969, 75).

A distinguished Scottish scientist felt that "the use of green light is dangerous unless skillfully applied" (Haverstock 1969, 75).

If there are several references to the same author and date, a short title can be added in each, or the forms 1969a, 1969b, and so on are used. A distinguishing initial would be added to the name only if for example two Haverstocks were cited.

The parenthetical-note form of citation requires a section, "References," at the end of the text to give complete information about the items. Behavioral scientists and natural scientists favor (insist on) using this system. If the book is a collection of papers by different authors, an individual reference section often appears at the end of each chapter.

The copyeditor must check every parenthetical citation in the text against the References to see that (a) the reference is indeed there, (b) that the author's name is spelled the same way (not Radford/Redford), and (c) that the dates given jibe.

BIBLIOGRAPHIES (AND NOTES)

A bibliography is consonant in form and style with the accompanying notes, but entries are fully expanded, usually with less abbreviation. Here is the place to give all pertinent information about the citation, sometimes including annotation. After first checking the alphabetization of the bibliography, the editor should confirm that details in the footnotes and bibliography agree. (See "Notes and Bibliography or References" in Chapter 5, "Editorial Procedures.")

The most common form of bibliography, particularly for those of modest size, is a listing of entries arranged alphabetically by author's last name. So the first and last names of the author or principal author are inverted.

Midgley, Mary. "Is Moral a Dirty Word?" *Philosophy* 47 (1972).

Note that the question mark in the title substitutes for the punctuation that would customarily follow the title and that no comma comes before the volume number, which is in arabic.

If a publication has more than one author, only the name of the first-mentioned author is inverted.

Wakefield, Walter, and Austin P. Evans. *Heresies of the High Middle Ages*. New York, 1969.

Note that the publisher is omitted here—which is OK if done consistently.

When the publisher is given, the form varies slightly. Occasionally publishers on both sides of the Atlantic are mentioned.

Benedict, Ruth. *Patterns of Culture*. Boston: Houghton Mifflin, 1934; London: Routledge and Kegan Paul, 1935.

A bibliography that is strictly alphabetical throughout is often the most helpful. Longer and more complicated bibliographies are sometimes organized by categories, in logical rather than alphabetical order, such as Books, Articles, Archival Sources, or by subject matter, as Trees, Plants, Shrubs, with alphabetical listings under each. The "Annotated Bibliography" in the present book is organized alphabetically under categories, with comprehensive annotation. (See more in "Alphabetization," below.)

REFERENCES (AND PARENTHETICAL CITATIONS)

References keyed to parenthetical notes in the text must be handled differently. The date is given more prominence since it helps to identify the item. The forms vary as to abbreviations, punctuation, italics, and lowercase or capital letters, but one form must be chosen and followed consistently. Abbreviations are common:

> Kelly, D. E. 1962. Pineal organs: Photoreception, secretion, and development. Am. Scientist 50:597.

Note two initials, date up front, no quotes around title, only first word capped, journal title in roman, no punctuation before volume number, no space between colon and page number.

> Urban, D. 1970. Raccoon population, movement patterns and predation on a managed waterfowl marsh. J. Wildlife Mgmt. **34**:372–82.

Note only one initial, though not preferred, no italics, boldface volume number. Boldface or italic volume numbers are unusual, but do not change them without the author's consent as they are customarily used by some scientists.

One way of distinguishing between two reports by one author in the same year is to add letters to the date in the textual reference and in the list of references.

> Holmes, J. R. 1960a. A preliminary report on the use of I[131]-labeled rose-bengal as a liver function test in sheep. *Cornell Vet. 50:*308–318.

> ———. 1960b. The application of radioisotopes as diagnostic aids in veterinary medicine. *J. Am. Vet. Med. Ass. 136:*309–317.

Note italic journal title and volume numbers. Repetition of the author's name is commonly avoided by using a 2-em or 3-em dash, the length depending on the house style or the designer's preferences.

Kare, M. R. 1965. The special senses. In *Avian Physiology*, ed. P. D. Sturkie. Cornell University Press, Ithaca, N.Y. Pp. 406–446.

————. 1967. Taste and food intake in domesticated and jungle fowl. *J. Nut.* 92:191–96.

Do not use a dash when another author is added in the next entry, but the dash can be used to stand for several authors when they are exactly the same in the entry following.

In the examples above, titles of journals are italic in some forms and roman type in others. Scientists who use many italicized Latin terms in their material often prefer titles in roman. Volume numbers show up as plain arabic numerals (most often), or arabic italics, or arabic boldface (rarely). And the place of publication in one follows mention of the publisher.

Your task is to see to it that only one general form is followed throughout.

PAGE AND VOLUME NUMBERS

In citing consecutive page numbers following 10, 20, 100, 200, and so forth, the first digits are always repeated: 10–11, 20–22, 100–101, 200–234. But 110 is followed by 11, 220 by 21, and so on. For other page numbers the choice is between the form 22–24 and 22–4 and between 222–24 and 222–4. Either system is acceptable, although some stylists do not like the single digit tacked on. The editor's job is to make the citations consistent. If the author is inconsistent, a timesaving option is to select the form that appears to require fewest editorial changes, or you can save space by going with the simpler form if it gives enough information.

Although current usage strongly favors the use of arabic instead of roman for volume numbers, I would rather not argue with an author who determinedly wishes to use a dozen or more roman numerals. But I would argue when an author neglects to supply dates for some entries, or gives a publisher for only some references, or attributes to Plato a book by Aristotle.

ALPHABETIZATION

In alphabetizing, many writers prefer the letter-by-letter system (considering all letters to the first mark of punctuation but ignoring hyphens and spaces). The word-by-word system is also acceptable. But the systems cannot be combined; you must follow one consistently. Remember that nothing comes before something in alphabetizing. And beginning articles in titles are usually ignored. (See also "Notes and Bibliography or References" in Chapter 5, "Editorial Procedures.")

For assistance with quirky forms and with handling documents and other unusual sources, check the various manuals of style, which give precise information on a myriad of possible forms. (The "Annotated Bibliography" advises on where to look for what.)

SUMMARY ON DOCUMENTATION

Abbreviations are widely used especially in notes. (See Figure 3 in the Appendix.)

Overall it is usually feasible, even necessary, to go along with the style chosen by your historian or literary critic; your chemist, psychologist, physicist, or veterinarian; your social scientist; or your legal scholar. The discipline of the subject customarily dictates usage.

Further guidance is to be found in the section "Basic Serviceable Forms of Notation and References," below, and in the books listed in the "Annotated Bibliography" under "Manuals on Grammar and Format." Scholarly and scientific journals also are useful models for the disciplines they represent.

When an author has used an acceptable form in notes and bibliography *consistently*, hesitate before you change everything to another form, however preferable it may seem. The changes may not be worth your time or a hassle with the author.

BASIC SERVICEABLE FORMS OF NOTATION
AND REFERENCES

Numbered Notes and Bibliography

In books, among the many acceptable variations, here is a standard serviceable style for numbered notes with superscripts in the text.

Notes—first mention

A REPRINT

> 1. Henry A. Myers, *Are Men Equal? An Inquiry Into the Meaning of American Democracy* (New York: Putnam's, 1945; reprint, Ithaca, N.Y.: Cornell University Press, Great Seal Books, 1955), 100–101, 104–5.

Note that the question mark takes the place of the customary colon before the subtitle. Observe also the consecutive page numbers. House style at some publishers calls for prepositions of two or more syllables or of five or more letters to be capped in a title.

MULTIPLE AUTHORS

> 2. Henry Higgins and James Myers, *To Be a Matador* (London: Kimber, 1972), pt. 3.

REVISED EDITION WITH ADDED INFORMATION

> 3. Bruno Nettl, *Folk Music in the United States: An Introduction*, 3d ed., rev. and enl. Helen Myers (Detroit: Wayne State University Press, 1976), 117–18.

The university press publishers are spelled out in this system, and notice the abbreviations.

BOOK IN A SERIES

> 4. Helen Myers, *Music of Hindu Trinidad: Songs from the India Diaspora*, Studies in Ethnomusicology (Chicago: University of Chicago Press, 1998).

The series title is cited with initial caps and no quotes.

BOOK IN PRESS

> 5. Jim Myers, *Afraid of the Dark: What Whites and Blacks Need to Know About Each Other* (Chicago: Lawrence Hill Books, in press).

This citation means that the book is at a publisher in process of composition or being printed.

ARTICLE IN A BOOK

> 6. Henry A. Myers, "Literature, Science, and Democracy," in *The Province of Prose*, ed. W. R. Keast and R. E. Streeter (New York: Harper, 1956), 682–92.
>
> 7. Henry A. Myers, "*Romeo and Juliet* and *A Midsummer Night's Dream*: Tragedy and Comedy," in William Shakespeare, *A Midsummer Night's Dream*, ed. Wolfgang Clemen (New York: New American Library, Signet Classics, 1963), 155–70.

ARTICLE IN MULTIVOLUME WORK

> 8. Helen Myers, "Ethnomusicology," in *The New Grove Dictionary of American Music*, 4 vols., ed. H. Wiley Hitchcock and Stanley Sadie (London: Macmillan, 1986), 2:58–62.

Note volume number, colon, no space, page numbers.

ARTICLE IN A JOURNAL

> 9. Helen Myers, "The Process of Change in Trinidad East Indian Music," *Journal of the Indian Musicological Society* 9 (Sept. 1978): 11–16.

Note journal, no punctuation, volume number, date in parens (OK if author says it's helpful, but use consistently for this journal), colon, page numbers. Note that space before page numbers is omitted if only a volume number is provided.

ARTICLE IN A NEWSPAPER

> 10. Jim Myers, "Little League Turns 50: Hometown Heroes 'Here' to Have Fun," *USA Today*, June 6, 1989, sec. A.

The newspaper date is given, but no page numbers.

ARTICLE IN PERIODICAL WITH NO VOLUME NUMBER

11. Henry A. Myers 4th, "The Phoenix and the Turtle," *Grapevine: Tompkins County's Weekly*, June 1–7, 1989, 7.

Date and page are given, using commas. You have to rest with this form if the periodical does not use volume numbers. But when volume numbers are available, ask the author to supply them, particularly if other volume numbers are given.

BOOK REVIEW

12. Helen Myers, review of *The Singing Tradition of Child's Popular Ballads* by B. H. Bronson, *The Musical Times*, May 1978, 419–20.

Month, year, and pages are given here, using commas.

DISSERTATION

13. Henry A. Myers, "An Introduction to the Timely and Synoptic Elements of Metaphysics," Ph.D. diss., Cornell University, 1933.

The title of an unpublished work is in quotes, not italics.

Subsequent references (the minimum necessary to identify an item)

14. Henry Myers, *Are Men Equal?* 21–22.

Several authors have this last name so first name is used also, and since there is more than one reference by this author a short title is used.

15. Higgins and Myers, 161–62.
16. Nettl, 109–10.
17. Henry Myers, "Literature, Science, and Democracy," 682.
18. Helen Myers, "Ethnomusicology," 62; Nettl, 104–5; Higgins and Myers, 70–71.

Combining several notes into one at the end of a paragraph, using semicolons between the items, can simplify notation.

Bibliography

Higgins, Henry, and James Myers. *To Be a Matador*. Foreword by Kenneth Tynan. London: Kimber, 1972.

Myers, Helen. "Ethnomusicology." In *The New Grove Dictionary of American Music*. Edited by H. Wiley Hitchcock and Stanley Sadie. 4 vols. London: Macmillan, 1986.

——. *Music of Hindu Trinidad: Songs from the India Diaspora*. Studies in Ethnomusicology. Chicago: University of Chicago Press, 1998.

——. "The Process of Change in Trinidad East Indian Music." *Journal of the Indian Musicological Society* 9 (Sept. 1978): 11–16.

——. Review of *The Singing Tradition of Child's Popular Ballads* by B. H. Bronson. *The Musical Times*, May 1978, 419–20.

Myers, Henry A. *Are Men Equal? An Inquiry Into the Meaning of American Democracy*. New York: Putnam's, 1945; reprint, Cornell University Press, Great Seal Books, 1955.

——. "An Introduction to the Timely and Synoptic Elements of Metaphysics." Ph.D. Diss., Cornell University, 1933.

——. "Literature, Science, and Democracy." In *The Province of Prose*, edited by W. R. Keast and R. E. Streeter. New York: Harper, 1956.

——. "*Romeo and Juliet* and *A Midsummer Night's Dream*: Tragedy and Comedy." In William Shakespeare, *A Midsummer Night's Dream*, edited by Wolfgang Clemen. New York: New American Library, Signet Classics, 1963.

Myers, Henry A., 4th. "The Phoenix and the Turtle." *Grapevine: Tompkins County's Weekly*, June 1–7, 1989.

Myers, Jim [James]. *Afraid of the Dark: What Whites and Blacks Need to Know About Each Other*. Chicago: Lawrence Hill Books, in press.

——. "Little League Turns 50: Hometown Heroes 'Here' to Have Fun." *USA Today*, June 6, 1989.

Nettl, Bruno. *Folk Music in the United States: An Introduction*. 3d ed. Revised and enlarged by Helen Myers. Detroit: Wayne State University Press, 1976.

Parenthetical Notes and References

The sources given above as numbered notes could be inserted into the text at convenient places as source notes or parenthetical references.

This system is generally preferred in the social and physical sciences, although the natural scientists have their own variants.

(H. A. Myers 1955, 100–101, 104–5)
(Higgins and Myers 1972, Pt. 3)
(Nettl 1976, 117–18)
(Helen Myers 1978a, 9:12)
(Higgins and Myers 1972, 201–2; Nettl 1976, 41–42)
(Higgins and Myers 1972, Nettl 1976)

The order is: author's name (just enough to identify), year of publication, comma, page numbers (or volume, colon, pages).

The corresponding list of references is arranged alphabetically. The year of publication follows the author's name, as these two items identify the source note in the text.

Higgins, Henry, and James Myers. 1972. *To Be a Matador*. London: Kimber.

Myers, H. A. 1933. "An Introduction to the Timely and Synoptic Elements of Metaphysics." Ph.D. diss., Cornell University.

———. 1955. *Are Men Equal? An Inquiry Into the Meaning of American Democracy*. New York: Putnam, 1945; reprint, Ithaca, N.Y.: Cornell Univ. Press, Great Seal Books.

———. 1956. "Literature, Science, and Democracy." In *The Province of Prose*, edited by W. R. Keast and R. E. Streeter. New York: Harper.

———. 1963. "*Romeo and Juliet* and *A Midsummer Night's Dream*: Tragedy and Comedy." In William Shakespeare, *A Midsummer Night's Dream*, edited by Wolfgang Clemen. New York: New American Library, Signet Classics.

Myers, H. A. 4th. 1989. "The Phoenix and the Turtle." *Grapevine: Tompkins County's Weekly*, June 1–7.

Myers, Helen. 1978a. "The Process of Change in Trinidad East Indian Music." *Journal of the Indian Musicological Society* 9 (Sept.): 11–16.

———. 1978b. Review of *The Singing Tradition of Child's Popular Ballads* by B. Bronson. *The Musical Times*, May, 419–20.

———. 1986. "Ethnomusicology." In *The New Grove Dictionary of*

American Music. Edited by H. W. Hitchcock and Stanley Sadie. 4 vols. London: Macmillan.

———. 1998. *Music of Hindu Trinidad: Songs from the India Diaspora.* Studies in Ethnomusicology. Chicago: Univ. of Chicago Press.

Myers, Jim [James]. 1989. "Little League Turns 50: Hometown Heroes 'Here' to Have Fun." *USA Today,* June 6.

———. In press. *Afraid of the Dark: What Whites and Blacks Need to Know About Each Other.* Chicago: Lawrence Hill Books.

Nettl, Bruno. 1976. *Folk Music in the United States: An Introduction.* 3d ed. Revised and enlarged by Helen Myers. Detroit: Wayne State Univ. Press.

You will encounter variants of these forms:

(a) In article titles: no quotes and lowercase for all words except initial caps.

(b) In journal and book titles: caps as usual but no italics. Or the ultimate simplicity: lowercase roman except for the first word in all titles and for proper nouns.

Hughes, C. C. 1957a. Reference group concepts in the study of a changing Eskimo culture. *In* Cultural stability and cultural change: Proceedings of the 1957 annual spring meetings of the American Ethnological Society, ed. V. F. Ray.

Note that an italic *In* is required here.

———. 1957b. An Eskimo deviant from the "Eskimo" type of social organization. American anthropologist 60:1140–47.

Note consecutive page numbers.

Whatever style is on tap, consistency can be your contribution. In notes and references and bibliographies, inconsistencies are deplorable. Perfection is the goal.

TEN

Special Editing Problems

Everybody in this world has problems. So you can expect that as copy-editors on the job you will have problems—frustrations, annoyances, disappointments, difficulties, questions.

AUTHORS' FOIBLES

Yet it is well worthwhile to have a go at figuring how to respond to whatever the author dishes up. Indeed getting along with authors is a principal part of your job, mainly persuading authors to let you help them.

Faulty Research

You may be assigned to edit articles accepted for publication by the editorial board of a journal. Suppose one of the articles is based on faulty research—a questionnaire distributed to 4-H Club youngsters at a conference. The subject of the questionnaire is bed sharing—with siblings, parents, grandparents, or others.

From this research the author has drawn some rather wide-ranging conclusions; the statistical analysis too looks faulty. Also maybe the teenagers questioned were pulling somebody's leg. Should such work be taken seriously?

But it is not for you at this point to suggest stringent revising or discarding the piece. You then might consider, though, that the print run for the journal is to be thousands of copies. Better see what you can do.

What can you do? First, query a few of the questionnaire answers that look like possible gags, and suggest not drawing conclusions from them. Next, attempt to make the language more precise, while describing research based on a relatively small sample, a sample that had not been scientifically selected. This kind of editing may result in the author's claiming less for the study. Take, for example, the assertion:

"Answers to Question 4 show that children . . ."

Change *show* to *suggest*, and the author seems less naive.

From such an experience you can take comfort in the thought that an idea clearly expressed can then make its way in the marketplace; the clearer the expression, the better can one judge its validity and appropriateness. From this point of view you can feel comfortable with the knowledge of all the half-baked ideas you may have helped along.

Stubborn Author

With luck you seldom will have to assist an author who is a fool. More often you will work with able professionals, experts who have something of consequence to say. Even with professionals, however, you may have some frustrating experiences. Relationships can become strained. You can be stymied by an author who is so sure of himself that he'll never consult a dictionary or by an author who is so fond of the sound of her own words that she is contemptuous of advice in style manuals. It is exasperating to be prevented from making surefire improvements that anyone but this author would recognize as welcome.

In such instances spend the time and effort to make several serious tries, or invoke authorities, to convince the author; but, if thwarted, you will have to be philosophical about goodness and perfection in this world. (How we wish that even our dearest friends were more nearly perfect!)

Equanimity in the face of bad writing does not come easily. But the mature person will aim steadfastly for editorial calm, a live-and-let-live, you-can't-win-them-all stance. Besides, you and your publishing house must always aim to stay on good terms with your authors.

Venerable Author

When dealing with a venerable author make clear that you know of the author's considerable accomplishments and that your suggestions are being made with no lack of respect. The question form is good for phrasing suggested changes or initiating revisions: "Hasn't this been said before?" "Do you mean 'always' or 'almost always'?" "Isn't this a cliché?"

Problem Prefaces and Introductions

Some writers have difficulty getting ready to pitch. The first few paragraphs may be only a false windup, while often the genuine first pitch of the book is on page 2. Other authors may endeavor to write a flossy opening to put their perspective in a worldview. Yet a crisp, sharp beginning may be at that place where they plunge into the terminology of their discipline. You should not assume that an author will not recognize the flaws in the opening if they are pointed out.

Another kind of flabby introduction begins with some details that are important to the writer but irrelevant and boring to the reader:

> The basic thesis of this book first occurred to me as I was walking along the shores of Lake Michigan one spring evening at sunset.

Then you have the task of suggesting gently that the sentence be deleted on the grounds that, although the occasion may have been memorable to the writer, it does not clarify the origin of ideas in the book or help the reader to understand.

Prefaces in which the author concentrates on telling what the book is not—and often neglects to say what it is—are especially disappointing. Usually the excuses offered in these negatives had better be left out:

Space limitations prevent adequate coverage of all aspects of the cluster fly's life cycle.

Yet the manuscript is already eight hundred pages long.

The publisher's limitations on space prevent inclusion of all the supporting evidence on tribal taboos.

Yet the book will have two hundred charts and tables.

This book will not answer some of the questions often asked about Moravians.

How frustrating!

This essay will not present textual analysis of the corpus of Wordsworth's work, nor will it delineate the influence of the poet's life on his work, nor dwell on the history of Wordsworth criticism, nor offer a new interpretation of Wordsworth's poetry.

What does it do? Even if the author goes on to state a purpose, the negatives add nothing.

Can't we say that criticism of publishers and other asides in prefaces had better be eliminated? Yes we can.

Another flaw sometimes found in introductory matter is that in describing the book the author merely repeats the wording of chapter titles. Ask the author to provide instead a summary, preferably in more detail or from an overall view, perhaps omitting chapter numbers altogether.

SPECIAL CASES

The questions that come up in copyediting, it would seem, might be concerned with matters of fact or with rules—that is, with conventions of usage or logic or practicality. But these problems are not always rulebook simple.

Lectures to Books

Lecturers normally do not read chapters of a book. When they do and the audience senses that part of a book is being read aloud, interest lags. A lecture needs immediacy, a spark, spontaneity; eye contact is a plus; gestures are important. Repetition of sorts is not necessarily bad. The chapters of a book can also sparkle with spontaneity, but the force of eye contact and gestures must be achieved by words, their order, the logic of their connections, and their sound to the mind's ear. Repetition is much more obvious since the words have not died on the air but remain on the printed page.

Readers do not wish to be addressed in a book as though they were sitting in a lecture hall. So delete references to "your happy faces," to "this evening," and to "topics to be discussed on another evening." The proceedings of a society may need to be reported as they happened on the occasion. Publishing a series of lectures as a book, except in unusual circumstances, requires a different point of view, focusing on someone sitting with a book in the hand rather than on someone sitting in a hall listening to a speaker.

Multiple Authorship

When a book comprises chapters by a number of authors, you as editor probably will have to monitor the assorted styles of these contributors. Very likely a style sheet will not have been sent in advance to the contributors. Hence you will have to provide guidelines for style, particularly for notes and bibliography, and for standardization of spelling (Sir Walter Ralegh/Raleigh, rain forest/rainforest), italics, abbreviations, and so on. All the variations you find in a single-author manuscript are multiplied in a collection. Your guidelines must be accepted by all the authors, just as books in a series must conform to the style of the other books in the series.

A quick overview may reveal which contributor's styling will require the least editing. Usually you would opt for fewer rather than many changes. Or you may find it expedient to follow the writing style of the editor or compiler of the collection.

Transliteration

In many questions of form, choices are available. Take transliteration, for example. Writers range over the world in their study of history, peoples, and conditions. They must use foreign words and names to describe their findings, and these words and names must be transcribed into an alphabet their readers will recognize.

The call for characters other than Roman (such as Arabic, Chinese, Greek, Hebrew, Hindi, Russian, Sanskrit) requires special consideration. Many compositors do not have fonts for these characters. As a result, the choice of a compositor and perhaps the design of a book may be governed by a few foreign words. So, if a manuscript uses only a few words in a foreign alphabet, urge the author to transliterate these few.

But if diacritical marks are necessary, accents, bars, underdots, and the rest are available and add a measure of accuracy that linguists and other scholars will appreciate.

The customary spelling of some well-known names may differ in the transliteration system chosen. Chekhov, usually found in reference books among the Cs with a cross-reference to the Ts, is also spelled Tchekhov or Chekov, though the first of the three spellings is the most common. Tchaikovsky, usually found among the Ts with no cross-reference, is also spelled Tschaikovsky, Tschaikowsky, or Chaikovski, though the first of the four is most common. Some writers prefer to use familiar spellings of well-known names, even though these spellings do not conform with the system chosen.

All names—of persons, places, organizations, buildings, streets, and currency—should appear in roman type. Other transliterated words are generally italicized.

Most writers are willing to spell the anglicized forms of well-known names in the usual way. They don't wish their work to be unintelligible to a segment of possible readers. Some writers, on the other hand, are unwilling to deviate from the transliteration system they have chosen. Then what are you to do in the interests of communication? One solution is to persuade the author to include in the front matter a short section on transliteration and to give among the examples common names in the book that are spelled uncommonly.

Such help is essential where names are barely recognizable and is to be recommended even when common names are given in the generally accepted forms. If the author is balky, you can go ahead and prepare a note on transliteration and very likely will find that it is acceptable to the author.

Translations

Editors dealing with translations of books sometimes have problems over missing information, particularly with respect to scholarly apparatus. Publication data about a reference cited should include city, publisher, and year, for books; volume number and month plus year or volume number, issue number, and year, for most journals; or location and dates for conferences when papers presented are being cited. The translator may have to be urged to contact a possibly reluctant author for this information or to seek it in a library (or on the Internet). Indeed, a publisher might well warn authors that they will be receiving queries along these lines.

Everything in a note should be translated except titles, and sometimes even they need to be clarified. Then use italics or quotation marks only if the translated title is of a published work.

Sources for all direct quotations must be given, including full publication information and exact page references. Whenever possible, authors should use quotations from English-language originals or published English translations, rather than translate passages afresh.

Thus an editor may have to require of a translator more than a word-for-word rendering of a text. The publisher's representative may have to ask for cooperation of author and translator again in order to supply the appropriate scholarly background for publication.

SCHOLARSHIP

Calling for help in checking the fine points of a manuscript does pay off. Turning to specialists for advice anywhere and anytime can be recommended for all editors. Most experts are as close as the telephone. Libraries have reference departments, ready for the unusual question. I have found that people are generally willing to aid writers—strangers with a question.

University press editors enjoy an advantage in dealing with scholarly problems. They have at hand a valuable intellectual resource, the teaching staff of the university. Professors are usually pleased to give a word of advice to an editor at their university press. Such a contact is a plus for most teachers. (Editors also are of course happy to answer queries from the faculty.)

Hebrew and Other Scripts

In a manuscript on biblical history, the author had used an ancient Hebrew script for the name of God, Yahweh. In the half-dozen places it occurred, he had drawn the characters by hand. At each, if we followed his lead, special artwork would have to be supplied by the production department, because the Hebrew typefaces available to the printer did not include this ancient form.

The question for me as the editor was: is this antique script necessary? When I called the professor of Hebrew studies at the university and read one of the passages, carefully pronouncing the Hebrew characters of the word (having first looked up the Hebrew names of the hand-drawn characters), the learned professor cried out: "You are spelling it backwards! But you can certainly use modern Hebrew there." That was all the authority needed to convince the author.

As with Hebrew, so also with other languages. You don't need to be proficient in Greek or German or Russian or Arabic but need only to know enough to ask the right questions.

Authoritative Sources and Accuracy

Since scientific and scholarly research are the basis for many books, copyeditors are better off if they know a little about research procedures and problems: methods of gathering and analyzing data, the nature of scientific sampling, the use of authoritative editions as sources, the necessity for careful deciphering of handwriting on documents—again just enough to ask the right questions. These questions usually will be directed to the author.

The conscientious editor will encourage an author to recheck all calculations if the author has not already done so and of course to supply references for all research data.

The author also is responsible for the accuracy of quotations. In the progression from handwritten notes to first draft to final copy, errors are easily introduced, even by careful writers. You therefore will stress the absolute necessity of checking all quotations in the final copy that is to go to the typesetter, back to the originals. This is a must.

Final Checking

Here, if you can be persuasive, you may save an author from providing fodder for hostile reviewers. The period of final checking, just before the manuscript is to go to the printer, is always an effective time to invoke the chastening thought of possible unfavorable reviews.

Now is the time to warn the author in advance against making costly changes in proof. Many an editor has had an author reject certain changes in manuscript and then wish to make them in proof. Too late. Or having accepted changes the author wants to restore the original in proof. Again, too late. Only correction of errors is feasible in proof. You must try to convince the author of the need for change at the preproof stage.

The toughest kind of problem for an editor is an author who is positive the manuscript is flawless. This problem is worse if the author will not consider any suggestions. All hope is lost if in addition the author's feelings are hurt.

Take care to avoid becoming an enemy. Persevere to remain a friendly professional who is trying to help. And resist hurt feelings yourself, remembering that an author has much at stake.

The kind of problem I have found most engaging is when in page proof the author insists that something must be added. Then, occasionally, comes the editor's private pleasure: by deleting a word or two or three to make the new material fit in, the paragraph is actually much improved.

"Life ain't nothin' but trouble," a wise old man once said to me, "trouble—and satisfaction." Yes, editors, it's problems—and solutions.

ELEVEN

Proofs and Index

Contacts between editors and authors in the computer age can be direct, swift, and as frequent as necessary. E-mail provides a quick, informal link; computer disks can be replicated in a flash.

A few authors, writing chiefly for journals, review editing and make corrections themselves onscreen. Most often, the house editor or freelance editor inputs all author and editorial changes.

Editors working onscreen send one or two successive printouts (hard copy) to authors. The first, by some called the "redlined" version, at one house shows editorial deletions in gray screens, inserts in boldface within curly brackets, and queries as temporary footnotes at the bottom of the page. (At another house, deletions are shown crossed out and additions shaded.) To ensure that corrections are noticeable, authors are asked to use a colored pen or pencil when making changes on printout. Some editors prefer a red felt-tip pen.

Publishers sometimes, with complicated textual material, return a printout (the second) of the revised redlined script, giving the author an opportunity to verify that changes have been included and keyboarded properly. This printout is the electronic equivalent of galley proof. E-mail can now be used for exchanges between editor and author, thus shortening production time.

Some weeks after the production department has sent the edited disk or manuscript to the compositor/typesetter, a schedule for the arrival of proofs will come from the typesetter. The dates are forwarded to the author along with the date the proof is to be returned to you. Adequate but limited time (usually several weeks, depending on the length of the manuscript) is allowed for the proofreading. The author must keep to the schedule, for a delay at this point is a setback for all. (If an author is late in returning proof, the printer may schedule another job in its place, which can delay publication of the book. And a delay in publication can ruin marketing plans.)

Publishers routinely ask typesetters to go "directly into pages" except when the design or makeup is unusually complicated or when heavy changes or foreign-language quotations may need to be scrutinized. Omitting the galley-proof stage saves labor, but author and editor must keep in mind that extensive alterations are all the more difficult and expensive to make in pages.

Thus the author checks the edited manuscript once or twice (on printouts) and then reads galley and/or page proof from the printer. The author may, or most often does not, see the final corrected proof, after which no changes are to be made—except, rarely, for correction of gross error.

PROOFS

When page proofs (or galleys, if that stage has not been skipped) arrive at the press from the printer, the first task is to go through them to see whether there are queries from the typesetter that can be answered before proof is sent to the author. Even queries addressed directly to the author might best be answered rather than risk an awkward solution by the author at this late moment.

Next, considerable checking is called for. See that the page numbers (folios) are all accounted for and are numbered correctly. Check the Contents page against chapter numbers, titles, subheads, and page numbers of the text. Cross-check illustrations, charts, and tables and look at their placement with reference to any mention in the text. One always hopes to find the illustration or chart following but near the first mention in the text.

Give the front matter a final close reading.

Check hyphens at the ends of lines to make sure that words are correctly broken.

Then send the proofs and the original edited script to the author with (1) instructions for reading proof, preferably including a list of symbols for correcting proof (Figure 4 in the Appendix); (2) a warning about making only necessary changes; and (3) a reminder about keeping to the proof schedule. Also send a duplicate set of proofs for the author to use in making the index.

After the author returns the proof (we trust on time), carefully check all corrections. Everyone hopes that any problems can be solved without having to consult the author at length. But sometimes a telephone call or an e-mail exchange can help to keep the book on schedule.

Flag author's alterations with a circled AA in the margins of the proof if the author has not done so. Flag any corrections that the editor makes with a circled EA in the margin and any coding errors CE, so that the cost of these changes will not be counted against the author, who is usually permitted by contract to make without charge changes amounting to a small percentage of the cost of composition.

At page-proof stage, if an author's alteration changes the number of lines on a page (thus rendering it longer or shorter than the facing page), you *must* revise the altered lines or other lines on the page so as to retain the original length, or add to or subtract from the text of the facing page. This is a puzzle that must be solved. Assuming the alteration indicated by the author is the correction of an error (the only kind of change permitted at this stage), you cannot go back to the original wording and so must count the characters in the altered part and come up with about the same number of characters for the final version, taking account that letters such as *i* and *m* are of different widths. In extremis the facing page may have to be altered to match. Here the mechanics of page makeup will overrule conciseness and nicety of style.

Finally, all corrections have to appear on the disk, the master printout, or the proof, as the case may be.

For journals, the author may see the edited manuscript but not be asked to read proof (or even get to see it). For dictionaries and encyclopedias, the author may not see the edited manuscript but may see courtesy proof while the master set is read in the house. Practices vary according to the publisher's needs and the demands of scheduling.

You and the author must of course have memorized the signs for correcting proof—an easy chore since they are simple and logical. (See Figure 4 in the Appendix for proofreaders' marks.)

Before turning over the page proof (with the original manuscript, which is kept as a document of record) to the production department, you may refer again to the checklist for copyeditors, this time to the sections on proof.

Sample Checklist for Copyeditors: Page-Proof Stage

Date pages received _____ Date to author _____
Date returned from author _____

_____ 1. Library of Congress number supplied.

_____ 2. Front matter read again.

_____ 3. First words of chapters, etc., OK if special design.

_____ 4. Folios OK.

_____ 5. Running heads OK.

_____ 6. Contents (including page numbers) checked against chapter and part titles and subheads if any.

_____ 7. Legends and numbers of figures, charts, illustrations, etc., OK.

_____ 8. Placement of tables, figures, charts, illustrations, etc., OK.

_____ 9. Footnote numbering OK.

_____ 10. Heads and subheads OK.

_____ 11. Extracts (style, spacing, etc.) OK.

_____ 12. Alphabetization of bibliography OK.

_____ 13.   Printer's queries and oddities in design called to attention of production department.

Date returned to production _____.

Ask production about revises or courtesy proof.

(If galley proofs have been sent to you and on to the author, the appropriate steps on this checklist are taken and at the page-proof stage are repeated.)

INDEX

The manufacturing schedule of a book usually calls for the index copy to go to the typesetter along with the corrected page proof, so the author generally is requested to send copy for the index manuscript when the pages are returned. Whether the author or a professional indexer is to prepare the index, you might well send the author an appropriate sample index.

Compiling an Index

The author who has just written a good book and is perhaps weary after checking quotations, page numbers, dates, and references, as well as the consistency of citations and of spellings, abbreviations, and punctuation—everything—this person may not be thrilled to hear the publisher's next pleasantry: "A good book deserves a good index. After proofreading do schedule plenty of time to work on an index."

So let's ask: "What's good about an index? What are we aiming at?"

The aim should govern the effort. The indexer and later the editor must focus on the people who will use this index. First come those who have read the book and wish to review information or comments they like, or dislike, or want to use. These readers need entries for the major topics discussed, including ideas, which may be the author's special contribution.

Next come those who are not going to read the entire book but wish to check on or learn about a subject possibly included there. So any topic that is discussed (not just mentioned in passing) should appear in the index. And in a book on east Indian music in Trinidad, for example, an item may need to appear in several forms, as "childbirth, songs at," or later "sohar," or again "songs: at childbirth" to cue in researchers.

Overall, the question "Will anyone look this up here?" can be a governing standard of what the editor can expect to be included. A good index gives a random picture of the book without the logical order and details, without connectives and grace notes, and with repetition (as in the childbirth songs). Entries should be concise rather than discursive, hit the center of an idea without tangents, supply the key word or words only. Better use nouns, few adjectives, probably no verbs or adverbs.

The proof schedule allows no time for the author to review index editing and very little time for editing, so a minimum of editing is preferable, although some most likely will be required.

Editing an Index

After processing the pages, you read the index. Every word and mark of punctuation is examined. The form in general is reviewed. The alphabetization is checked, and an extra line space is usually marked before the beginning entry of each letter in the alphabet. Once again consistency is the goal, as well as economy of space.

Cross-references are used in indexes to save space, and all of them need to be checked by you. When an entry such as "Captions" is discussed on pages under another entry, a cross-reference such as "(*see* Legends)" is used in a good index if, and only if, it will take less space than the page numbers. You can check that the cross-reference matches the entry word for word, but if the reference does not save space, supply page numbers instead. (Index items may or may not have initial caps.)

Sometimes additional relevant information on the subject of an entry is given elsewhere, justifying a cross-reference such as "(*see also* Headings)" if, and only if, at least one additional page number appears. When only one or two new pages are given under a cross-reference and the connection between the entries is close, the numbers can be added to the principal entry and the cross-reference deleted. If, on the other hand, you reckon that some readers might not look for *pigeons* under *doves* (where pigeons are listed), add an entry: "Pigeons, *see* Doves."

In general everything should be in alphabetical order, or chronological order if dates are listed. Hyphens are marked as in regular text copy; caps, italics, and other spellings as in the rest of the book. The faithful copyeditor can help by controlling formal consistency, by eliminating trifling entries, and by adding any major topics that have eluded the indexer. For examples of forms and punctuation, refer to, especially, the following index entries in the present book: Authors, Checklists for copyeditors, Figures, Footnotes, and Source notes.

Sample Checklist for Copyeditors: Index Copy

_____ 1. Printer told page number on which to begin Index.

_____ 2. Alphabetization of entries OK, either letter by letter or word for word but not a mixture.

_____ 3. Order of subentries either alphabetical or chronological— not a mixture of both.

_____ 4. Space between letter breaks marked.

_____ 5. Cross-references checked: that there *is* an entry; that the entry itself is the same as the cross-reference.

_____ 6. All inclusive/consecutive page numbers are in the form selected.

_____ 7. Use of *see* and *see also* properly done.

_____ 8. Check that there is no punctuation immediately following entries.

FINALE

At this point in the manufacturing process, you will pause, because here is virtually the last chance to correct errors. Also at this moment the mass of materials is beginning to look like a book. So you glance back with some apprehension to make sure everything is OK and ahead with some satisfaction to the appearance of a new item for bookstores and libraries.

Next there may be index proof to read.

Then digital blues, complete prints from the electronic files of the entire book, may show up. At this stage you will examine places where something was changed at the last moment, make sure the charts and illustrations are right side up and sited as intended—in sum, everything in place.

Next the pages of the actual book before binding (folded and gathered sheets—also called "f & gs") have to be looked at. And then boards for the binding (sample stamped case, the actual hardcover to go on the book) may come to you with stamping of the author's name, the title, and the publisher to be carefully checked.

The sample checklists are simple.

Index proof

_____ 1. Read against copy.

_____ 2. Folios OK; index begins where it should.

_____ 3. Running heads OK.

Digital blues and/or folded and gathered sheets

_____ 1. Folios OK.

_____ 2. Everything right side up.

_____ 3. Illustrations in place.

Finally, you are handed a copy of the finished book. Let's hope that a close examination will reveal nothing wrong. Then you experience the pleasure of being a copyeditor. One's work endures.

TWELVE

Job Satisfaction

Copyediting can provide a competent person with a modest livelihood in an interesting, relatively secure, comfortable, but not monotonous job. Copyediting does not always pay well and is frequently tedious, requiring hours of concentration. Yet many people, like the faithful, persevering mail carrier, are satisfied to make a career of it whether the going is rough or smooth.

OPPORTUNITIES

Copyediting also can lead somewhere. The opportunities are varied and challenging. The copyeditor can move on to become an acquisitions editor. In this job, the ability to size up a manuscript is important. Facility in assessing the potential of an idea, in judging the possible market for a book, and in seeing the weakness of a presentation qualifies an editor for such a position. Aptitude for dealing with people also helps.

Some experienced copyeditors become managing or executive editors. These positions of course require organizing ability and planning skills. Attention to detail and to the overall scene is necessary: an interest in people and a gift for judging people is useful, as well as some notion of future possibilities for the publishing house.

A few good copyeditors, particularly at the university presses, move from editor to a higher management position, say, editor-in-chief or director. They have the larger view, understanding of the business side of the publishing scene, some ideas about where their press could go, and in the top jobs what we might call personality.

In the large commercial houses as well, opportunities are offered to move from straight copyediting to supervisory positions.

In the textbook field, too, mobility is offered in the development of series for courses and in coordinating the books being manufactured to the needs of the schools.

Several copyeditors I know moved on to become editors-in-chief for a corporation's in-house organ. These persons find the job exhilarating; they are in charge. Opportunity and money are available for first-class publications.

Editors are needed in museums to prepare booklets for exhibits and to organize reports on acquisitions and future programs.

Editors are needed on countless journals, in such general subjects as art and music and in such specialized subjects as model-plane building or beekeeping or historic preservation. Editing for journals of science, law, medicine, and many other disciplines may or may not require familiarity with the subject. Well-paying positions show up on this front. Business organizations, religious groups, physical fitness clubs—you name it—all sponsor weekly or monthly or quarterly publications for their members. Newsletters are in vogue, on computer currents, musicology, mental health, and so forth.

Alumni magazines offer opportunities for editors. Graduates have an inside track there.

Editing on a dictionary or encyclopedia generally requires some writing skills. Here is an opportunity for contributing to especially worthy projects.

A person with a good command of English who is willing to take pains and to assume the job of supervising the writing of reports or proposals is welcome everywhere—in government, in business, in marketing, on Wall Street, in nonprofit organizations that must address the public, as well as at publishers large and small.

REWARDS

Many publishers prefer freelancers these days to in-house editors. For the couple who wish to give time to raising a family, freelance editing at home for either partner provides the freedom necessary for such balancing. I know a number of young people who continued to contribute their editing skills at home while raising a family. Part-time freelance editing was a boon during complicated, busy periods in their lives. Later, full-time freelance work remained an option.

As writers and publishers rely more and more on the computer's capacity to help, the temptation is to marvel at technology while taking advantage of the machine's checking capability and manuscriptwide survey techniques as well as the ability to turn out a good product in record time. An editor thus might indeed enjoy being on the so-called cutting edge of technology. Yet anyone in the publishing business cannot help but marvel also at the breadth and depth of the published work. One might say that almost every entry in *Webster's* unabridged dictionary has been written about by authors and made into a book by publishers. So an editor, in the middle, can enjoy being on the cutting edge also of projects and ideas.

Different people find different rewards in their jobs. For me the most profound pleasure has come from the knowledge that I am participating to a small degree in the intellectual life of our times. That small degree has brought great satisfaction. Some copyeditors might well feel that the measure of clarity, correctness, consistency, and conciseness they bring to the business is worth their toil. Others might revel in the contact with ideas or with people.

Copyediting is hardly just earning a living. The editors I know don't view it that way. If an article or a book contributes a little to knowledge of the world or to understanding of people or to enjoyment, and if the copyeditor of the book or article adds a small measure of clarity or correctness or verve to this view of the world or of people, then the editor, one who cares, has contributed a small measure of a little bit— enough.

Annotated Bibliography

DICTIONARIES

The number of dictionaries is astonishing, as is the number of new words in dictionaries. During the eighties, lexicographers added more than 40,000 new words from that decade, and during the nineties new words were added at the rate of more than 2,500 per year, with many new meanings for old words as well. Mind-boggling also is the latest method of disseminating bookish news; most recently electronic publishing and online sources of information have shocked old-time bibliophiles out of their library chairs.

Everyone touting a dictionary cites sources in vast electronic databases, and everyone is eager to have snared the very latest new word. Some old lexicographers boast their reliability. Purveyors of the newest dictionary boast its hurried-up usefulness with "quick definitions."

Since new editions have relied on electronic databases to update their entries, the bright future surely looks in that direction. One new approach, apparently abandoning traditional historical principles as a base, flaunts reliance on computer technology.

A trend is the renaming of successive editions by adding a word, as

Desk, or *College,* or *Webster,* which last now appears on half the dictionaries in bookstores. *Webster's Collegiate,* a descendant of the original Noah Webster, is using an older affiliation, Merriam-Webster, to distinguish itself.

A new tool for the editor checking a manuscript is the electronic dictionary. Following Microsoft's popular electronic *Encarta Encyclopedia,* the *Encarta World English Dictionary* in book form and electronically is being heavily advertised. Oxford is planning an online version of the twenty-volume *OED.* Other publishers are readying their electronic versions of the words in the English language, of other languages, and of encyclopedias. This activity is sure to be a boon to editors and writers and readers. We shall all become better informed, perhaps with less effort. We can hope the reliability quotient will be high.

The competing conventional concise dictionaries have expanded their offerings to include more entries and more extras in a manageable compass; type sizes are reduced but still readable. For about $25.00, in these judiciously crammed packages you can buy the world: almost all the useful words in the English language, biographical and geographical names, foreign words and phrases, abbreviations, a manual of style, lists of colleges and universities, tables of weights, measures, and everything else, with charts galore including ships bells and the Beaufort scale. What a world!

Because of the exploding language, an editorial office or a freelance editor will need one of the latest dictionaries, usually called a college, collegiate, or concise edition, as well as—somewhere—that essential companion, an unabridged dictionary of the English language.

Many choices are ready for you.

Unabridged Editions

American
Encarta World English Dictionary. New York: St. Martin's, 1999. xxxii + 2,078 pp.

Encarta is not the first to document English usage by using computer and database technology, but it is the first to rely principally on the current idiom as its base: 320 scholars in 20 nations worked for three years using e-mail to produce a "word corpus showing English in all its varieties worldwide" (p. ix)—over 400,000 references. In a bow to the way we live today ("in a hurry"), *Encarta* supplies "quick definitions," in boldface, to summarize the full definitions. This device results in considerable repetition:

> **abandon . . . 1.** *vt.* **LEAVE SOMEBODY BEHIND** to leave somebody or something behind for others to look after, especially somebody or something meant to be a personal responsibility. . . .

The Microsoft compilation will surely become a valuable source of information. But at present editors on the job, working to bring perfection to a manuscript, perhaps might heed the advice: "Be not the first by whom the new are tried." For numerous authorities as well as experts who have worked on this project criticize it: for errors (Gen. George Gordon Meade does not belong in the Revolutionary War; the Anglo-Saxon symbol *edth* is wrongly labeled), for bad judgment (in giving precedence to Madonna, the singer, over the Madonna, the mother of Jesus), and for haste (to meet the fall deadline of school openings). *Encarta*'s blurb about itself spurs a reader to look into this new dictionary for its definition of *hubris:*

> **hubris . . .** *n.* **1. PRIDE** excessive pride or arrogance **2. EXCESSIVE AMBITION** the excessive pride and ambition that usually leads to the downfall of a hero in classical tragedy [Late 19th C. From Greek.] . . .

Microsoft *Encarta,* with advertising superlatives, is trying to intimidate the heirs of Noah Webster. We on the sidelines doubtless will become beneficiaries of this encounter.

The Random House Webster's Unabridged Dictionary. Special 2d ed. New York: Random House, 1997. xxvi + 2,229 pp.

Updated from the database of the RH Living Dictionary Project, this volume gives much information under more than 315,000 entries: advice about italics and caps, abbreviations, usage, and etymologies.

Proper names include biographical and geographical information, organizations, historical events, and works of art, literature, and music. Included also are more than 50,000 new words and 75,000 new meanings. An eight-page new-words section lists the ballyhooed *yada yada yada* (first used 1940–45).

Extra bonuses are provided: dictionaries of French, Spanish, Italian, and German words, lists of signs and symbols, a useful "Basic Manual of Style," an excellent article on usage and change, a directory of colleges and universities, a world atlas (with maps), a gazetteer (keyed to the atlas), and much more historical and geographical information.

Webster's Third New International Dictionary of the English Language. Unabridged. Springfield, Mass.: Merriam-Webster, 1993. 2,663 pp.

When *Webster's Third* first appeared in 1961, some old-timers were disappointed that it did not take a stand on caps and italics (unlike the second edition, 1936). Its failure to do so may have reflected concerns that language and usage were changing too rapidly. With more than 460,000 entries, 200,000 usage examples, and an addendum of new words, though obviously not the newest latest, it has tried to keep abreast of the twentieth century's expanding vocabulary. Place names are included; names of persons come only under adjectival forms, where they appear as part of the definitions. *The New York Times* says it is the "closest we can get, in America, to the Voice of Authority." Any editorial office will have good use for it.

English

The Oxford English Dictionary. 2d ed. 20 vols. New York: Oxford University Press, Clarendon, 1989. Popularly referred to as the *OED*.

The twenty-volume *Oxford*, newly consolidated and updated, is the only dictionary that traces the development of a word from its first appearance, with examples of usage by famous authors through the centuries. A busy copyeditor will find it too cumbersome for daily use, but any word fancier of course will find its historical tracings fascinating.

Abridged Editions

American

The American Heritage Dictionary. 4th ed. Boston: Houghton Mifflin, 2000. 2,074 pp.

The fourth edition of this esteemed reference is a complete revision of the third, including new scientific and technical terms and added biographical and geographical names—over 200,000 entries in all. This edition shows more than 10,000 new words since 1992. Usage notes on language changes are included in boxes, and we hear again that usage dictates acceptability (but the usage panel hates *hopefully*). Small but readable print enables the publishers to squeeze their abridged volume along with more than 4,000 full-color illustrations into a smaller trim. A CD-ROM package is available.

Merriam-Webster's Collegiate Dictionary. 10th ed. Springfield, Mass.: Merriam-Webster, 1999, principal copyright 1993. xxxviii + 1,559 pp.

The tenth edition of the *Collegiate Dictionary* deserves its claim to be "The Voice of Authority." Based on *Webster's Third* and on a constantly updated file of English and American usage, the 1999 printing is thoroughly current. Editors will appreciate the many examples of good usage. Biographical and geographical names, foreign words and phrases, signs and symbols, and a handbook of style are included, in small but readable type. Incidentally, computer users have prevailed: *programmer* is now preferred. It boasts over 215,000 entries.

Microsoft Encarta College Dictionary. New York: St. Martin's Press, 2001. xli + 1,678 pp.

The *Encarta College* edition contains more than 320,000 entries, including 5,000 new words, many highly technical terms, and proper names and places. As a result of input by college professors, it has added "Correct Usage Notes" for such words as *apostrophe, possessive,* and *sort of.* Included also are some "Quick Facts," as for *Theater of the Absurd,* and some "Literary Links," as the one under *time* to Stephen Hawking's work.

Encarta lexicographers have judged that not all words deserve or lend themselves to Encarta's contribution, the "Quick Definition." Both *abandon* and *hubris* get the quick treatment in the *Encarta World* volume. But in the college edition, although *abandon* qualifies for a quick one, *hubris* does not. Errors that reviewers found in *Encarta World* have been corrected for the college edition.

Random House Webster's College Dictionary. New York: Random House, 1999. xxviii + 1,571 pp.

This abridged edition, updated annually, has more than 207,000 definitions, with biographical and geographical names integrated into the general listings. Derivations and first use are indicated, examples of offensive language explained—all in a good, readable typeface. In a special section, new words are listed by decades from the forties through the nineties. *Copyeditor* now is first choice, *copy editor* acceptable.

Webster's New World College Dictionary. 4th ed. New York: Macmillan, 1999. 1,716 pp.

The *New World Dictionary* runs over 1,700 pages. Of its 160,000 plus entries, over 7,000 are new terms—a special boon to editors. It stresses Americanisms and is widely used by American newspaper editors as well as other editors. It gives ample definitions, precise derivations, advice on italics, and help with syllabification. Biographical and geographical names are included in the overall listing. Synonyms are a specialty. The type is quite readable.

English
Chambers 21st Century Dictionary. Edinburgh: Chambers, 1996. x + 1,654 pp.

Although not well known in the United States, this dictionary is widely used in England. Editors rely on it. Its definitions are extraordinarily complete, including dates, derivations, and extensive illustrations of idiomatic usage. Slang, colloquialisms, foreign words and phrases used in English, U.S. meanings, and American spellings are given attention. Biographical and geographical names show up usually in adjectival form. A welcome unusual feature is the offering of "Plain English" alternatives to overpompous expressions: *"avail oneself of something* * Plain English alternatives are **use it, make use of it**" (p. 89). Here is England's unhurried antidote to, though predating, *Encarta*.

The Concise Oxford Dictionary of Current English. 9th ed. Oxford: Oxford University Press, 1995. xxi + 1,673 pp.

About the size and heft of *Merriam-Webster's Collegiate*, the ninth edition is 14 percent larger than the eighth, with over 7,000 new words. The Oxford editors are proud of its sources: the ongoing work on the twenty-volume *OED* and OUP's unique collection of electronic data. They note the trends away from using accents, hyphens, italics, and capitals. Under *black* a substantial passage on usage is to the point, along with many other good tips on usage throughout. For Americans they followed a special consultant for North American usage, giving one *l* in *traveled* as "US usu." The nicety of definition here is admirable, but you won't find Walter Mitty or Wampanoag Indians. A writer could find help in this Oxford volume; an American editor would choose *Merriam-Webster*.

DK Illustrated Oxford Dictionary. New York: Oxford University Press, 1998. 1,008 pp.

A new entry on the scene, the *Illustrated Oxford* is gorgeous and innovative, a volume anyone would love to own. For example, you have a piano not only pictured but with all its parts named, a lobster with all its parts dissected, the planet Mercury with its structure revealed, etc., etc. An editorial office could use this volume, but editors will have to forgo browsing.

The New Shorter Oxford English Dictionary. 4th ed. 2 vols. New York: Oxford University Press, 1993. 3,801 pp.

The New Shorter Oxford draws on the twenty-volume *OED*'s research program as well as a constantly updated database. Using a historical and literary approach, it follows changed meanings through history with quoted examples. It covers everywhere in the world where English is spoken. It contains 98,000 headwords, 83,000 illustrative quotations ranging from the Bible to Martin Luther King, some 500,000 definitions in all. Foreign terms and phrases, trade names, and changing meanings are given and U.S. spellings as well as British. It is not so informative regarding Americanisms as the U.S. volumes but is a jewel with respect to word meanings and usage.

Thesauruses

Most word-processing programs come with built-in thesauruses, which can be very handy during electronic editing. These are limited, however, and a print version is still a must.

Bartlett's Roget's Thesaurus. Boston: Little Brown, 1996. xxxii + 1,415 pp.

An editor searching for a synonym to replace an overworked word can readily find what's wanted in one of the latest thesauruses. *Bartlett's Roget* is comprehensive and easy to use.

Supplementary Volumes

Regional usage

A book published in Canada will silently subscribe to usage accepted in that country; books published in the United States will without question silently subscribe to U.S. practices. English publications generally suit Canadians, but some so-called Americanisms have become respectable up north. A number of reference books stress regional differences and give assistance in conforming to the practices and usage of wherever you are—Australia, Jamaica, Newfoundland, South Africa.

Foreign languages

An editorial office most likely will have use for standard dictionaries of French, German, Italian, and Spanish. Many other language dictionaries are available—from Hindi to Greek, Russian to Portuguese to

Swedish, from Native American tongues to Indian and Asian languages. Use of a foreign-language dictionary will often be on an elementary level; nevertheless such checking can be face-saving.

MANUALS ON GRAMMAR AND FORMAT

Comprehensive Manuals

The Chicago Manual of Style. 14th ed. Chicago: University of Chicago Press, 1993. x + 921 pp.

Some readers brought up on the King James version of the Bible have never quite warmed up to any Revised Version. But nobody has anything other than praise for the revised editions of the editor's bible, *The Chicago Manual.* The fourteenth edition builds on previous editions and is as usual authoritative and easy to use. A new revision is under way, so we can expect to read about changing usage and the latest style one of these days.

In this edition a generous number of examples are given; the role of computers is detailed, along with editing procedures on hard copy and online; the styling of notes and bibliography or references is treated extensively; and the changing contemporary usage for compound words is noted.

This manual is designed for editors. A beginning editor could study every page with profit. Anyone will find it useful for advice about punctuation, spelling, and abbreviations or for help with numbers, proper names, foreign languages, quotations, permissions, and tables. It gives excellent instructions on handling illustrative material. The sections on indexing and alphabetizing answer all questions.

It doesn't pretend to give advice about how to write.

Copy-Editing: The Cambridge Handbook for Authors, Editors, and Publishers. 3d ed. By Judith Butcher. Cambridge: Cambridge University Press, 1992. 483 pp.

Now in its third edition, revised and updated, this complete guide to British style and usage is an ever-present help for British editors and is not to be ignored by Americans. It deals with abbreviations, caps, italics, proper names, spelling, and punctuation and with front matter, headings, cross-references, notes, and bibliographical references. Admirable advice is given on numbers and on tables, appendixes, foreign languages, and quotations. Other details are not neglected, including dates, money, measurements, scientific and mathematical nomenclature, and special subjects such as classics, law, music. Processing of proof is explained, and the section on indexes is guaranteed to be useful. Suggestions are offered how to handle anything that might cause unnecessary difficulty, expense, or delay in production.

At other houses editing procedures and relations between editors and departments may differ from those at Cambridge University Press, but this book gives a coherent picture of the editor's place in the publishing process.

Merriam-Webster's Manual for Writers and Editors. Springfield, Mass.: Merriam-Webster, 1998. xiii + 424 pp.

Like Webster's dictionaries, this manual for authors and editors is based on continuous study of usage and on extensive citation files of English as used in books, newspapers, and magazines. It offers much detailed advice on the language, on using the computer in publishing, on foreign languages, on indexing, and other pertinent subjects.

MLA Handbook for Writers of Research Papers. 5th ed. Revised by Joseph Gibaldi. New York: Modern Language Association, 1999. xviii + 332 pp.

Although much of the advice about research papers will not apply to the publishing business, an editor might do well to know MLA recommendations if an author is following them and advise an author how to revise them for publication.

United States Government Printing Office Style Manual. Washington, D.C.: USGPO, 2000. x + 326 pp.

Most editors can bypass the tips about writing for government publications and turn to the advice about capitals, italics, hyphens, and compounds, about abbreviations, symbols, and numerals, about foreign words, and about punctuation. The manual supplies long lists of helpful examples.

Words into Type. 3d ed. Based on studies by Marjorie E. Skillin, Robert M. Gay, and others. Englewood Cliffs, N.J.: Prentice-Hall, 1974. xx + 586 pp.

This authoritative manual of style has been a standby in many editing offices for more than twenty-five years and is still available from bookstores. It gives information about copyright, libel, proofreading, and indexes; about abbreviations, symbols, numbers, weights, measures, italics, capitalization, spelling, scientific terms, proper nouns, and adjectives; about tables, notes, bibliography, captions, and foreign languages.

The sections on grammar, punctuation, and the use of words are clear and complete. The advice about tenses, sentence structure, and the position of modifiers leads the writer a step beyond correctness toward literary skill. The section on wordiness, trite expressions, circumlocutions, and foreign words also gives hints on writing well.

Regrettably, a projected fourth edition has been canceled.

Special Helps from Disciplines

Bias-free thinking

Miller, Casey, and Kate Swift. *The Handbook of Nonsexist Writing.* 2d ed. San Jose: iUniverse.com, 2001. x + 182 pp.

The authors of this lively discussion dissect historical usage in illuminating their thesis that language has supported sexist discrimination through the ages. They give a graceful, thoughtful account of efforts to remove such bias from current language. First-rate examples abound, many of them amusing. A few asides about race are to the point. Their perceptive arguments about language bias may prompt writers and editors to work harder to avoid or eliminate it.

Schwartz, Marilyn. *Guidelines for Bias-Free Writing*. Bloomington: Indiana University Press, 1995. xii + 100 pp.

A team appointed by of the Association of American University Presses compiled this guide to assist writers in avoiding unsuitable language with regard to gender, race, ethnicity, and sexual orientation, as well as concerning seniors and persons with disabilities. A bibliography shows where to look further.

Classical studies

The Oxford Classical Dictionary. 3d ed. London: Oxford University Press, 1996. 1,704 pp.

This tome supplies 6,000 clear, authoritative entries.

Law

Black's Law Dictionary. 7th ed. St. Paul, Minn.: West, 1999. 1,738 pp.

Bluebook: A Uniform System of Citation. 17th ed. Cambridge: Harvard Law Review Association, 2000. 300 pp.

Medicine

American Medical Association. *Manual of Style: A Guide for Authors and Editors.* 9th ed. Baltimore, Md.: Williams and Wilkins, 1998. 660 pp.

An essential handbook for medical/scientific writers, this edition includes an expanded chapter on legal and ethical issues in publishing.

Stedman's Medical Dictionary. 27th ed. Baltimore, Md.: Williams and Wilkins, 2000. 2,029 pp.

List of Journals Indexed in Index Medicus. Bethesda, Md.: National Library of Medicine, Bernan Associates. Published annually.

Sciences

Day, Robert A. *How to Write and Publish a Scientific Paper.* 5th ed. Phoenix: Oryx, 1998. 296 pp.

Editors will find here good advice on the editing of tables and on avoiding jargon in scientific writing, as well as the latest on electronic publishing in the sciences.

McGraw-Hill Dictionary of Scientific and Technical Terms. 5th ed. New York: McGraw-Hill, 1994. 2,194 pp.

This edition covers more than one hundred scientific fields from acoustics to zoology and can be installed on computers with one of several popular software programs.

Scientific Style and Format: The CBE Manual for Authors, Editors, and Publishers. 6th ed. Cambridge: Cambridge University Press, 1994. xv + 825 pp.

Almost tripled in size, this guide now covers the physical sciences and mathematics as well as the life sciences. Spelling, capitalization, the use of numbers, and more—both American and British preferences— are taken into account. CBE stands for Council of Biology Editors.

Online Style

Hale, Constance, and Jessie Scanlon. *Wired Style: Principles of English Usage in the Digital Age.* Rev. ed. New York: Broadway Books, 1999. vii + 198 pp.

Since *Wired Style* has been called "a *Chicago Manual of Style* for the millennium" (*Newsweek*) and "the Strunk and White for the digerati" (*Entertainment Weekly*), it invites the attention of serious stylists. Lively paced and daringly innovative, "it is written primarily for journalists" and hasn't "delved into the myriad questions facing authors writing in an academic context" (p. 183). The major portion of the book is a glossary, in which future usage is anticipated by omitting the hyphen in *e-mail.* Defined is *digerati*—"the digital elite." Not defined is *SGML*—the Standard Generalized Markup Language of generic coding. So one has to say this interesting, quirky book won't be of great help to editors in general.

Walker, Janice R., and Todd Taylor. *The Columbia Guide to Online Style.* New York: Columbia University Press, 1998. xvi + 218 pp.

The knowledgeable authors of this guide suggest forms of reference for every kind of computer source one could think of, using standard humanistic and scientific citations as a guide.

STYLISTIC AIDS ON WRITING

Basics

The Associated Press Stylebook and Briefing on Media Law. Edited by Norm Goldstein. Cambridge, Mass.: Perseus, 2000. vi + 413 pp.

This compendium for journalists lists useful trade names (e.g., Ford TriMotor), identifies the Seven Seas and the Seven Sisters, uses common sense for compounds (Italian-American and Mexican-American but French Canadian and Latin American), and warns that *fulsome* means disgustingly excessive. Abbreviations such as Jan. 3, sanctioned here, are not acceptable in formal prose.

Baker, Sheridan. *The Practical Stylist.* 8th ed. New York: Longman, 1997. 277 pp.

This study of the art of writing is packed with sound advice for any editor. A glossary of usage assembles almost all the mistakes an editor is likely to encounter. This edition includes help with description, narration, and exposition.

Cook, Claire Kehrwald. *Line by Line: How to Improve Your Own Writing.* Boston: Houghton Mifflin, 1985. xx + 219 pp.

The hardcover edition of this work was published under the title *The MLA's Line by Line: How to Edit Your Own Writing.*
Consistency, correct spelling, and rulebook grammar—these we notice automatically. But doesn't our best work often center on achieving clarity, uncluttered prose, and forthright communication? *Line by Line* (a good title) declares that after "styling mechanics" are out of the way "the copy editor devotes a separate close reading—or several readings

if time allows—to removing any obstacles to the clarity and grace of sentences" (p. xiv). What follows is pithy, exemplary advice for writers and editors: on baggy sentences, faulty connections, ill-matched partners, mismanaged numbers, and imprecise punctuation. Telling examples, of bad sentences and good, strengthen the argument. "A Glossary of Questionable Usage" supplies guidance on troublesome terms such as *who* and *whom, affect* and *effect*. A good read.

Fowler, Henry W. *A Dictionary of Modern English Usage*. 2d ed. Revised by Sir Ernest Gowers. Oxford: Oxford University Press, 1965; Oxford Paperback (with corrections), 1983. xxiv + 726 pp.

Much beloved, in both its original and second edition, Fowler's *MEU*, I must say reluctantly, now belongs to language history, for English has proceeded on its merry changing way during the more than seventy years since this schoolmaster first harangued us. But we still honor him, in part, as Gowers concluded, because "all kinds of affectation and humbug were anathema to his fastidious mind." We'll keep his book on our editor's shelf. The original Fowler (1926) is available, reprinted in 1994 by Wordsworth Editions. (See *The New Fowler's Modern English Usage*, below.)

The New Fowler's Modern English Usage. 3d ed. Edited by R. W. Burchfield. Oxford: Oxford University Press, Clarendon, 1996. xxiii + 864 pp.

An editor, who must deal with English usage daily, might well dip into this new *MEU*. Burchfield has devoted many years to this update and has given us a brave new lexicon distinguished as in its former life by erudition, panache, and wit. Amassing a huge store of examples, he has sampled English usage around the world and tells us what is going on now. Although bound by common usage, he does allow himself to be judgmental. He says that the forms *worth while, worth-while*, and *worthwhile* may be "legitimately used," but "the use of the solid form *worthwhile* in the predicative position (*the experiment was worthwhile*) is undesirable, though now regrettably common" (p. 857). So editors, and authors, you can be elitist (with Burchfield) or run with the crowd (as Webster).

Burchfield is generous with *hopefully* too and reckons that "any number of adverbs in *-ly* have come into common use as sentence adverbs" but also observes: "Conservative speakers, taken unawares by the sudden expansion of an unrecognized type of construction, have exploded with resentment that is unlikely to fade away before at least the end of the 20c" (p. 703).

Strunk, William, Jr. *The Elements of Style: With Revisions, an Introduction, and a Chapter on Writing by E. B. White.* 4th ed. Boston: Allyn and Bacon, 2000. xviii + 105 pp.

This edition bears a Foreword by Roger Angell (White's stepson), an Afterword by Charles Osgood, and an added Glossary and Index.

This slim guide tackles major problems of writing along with many common mistakes in grammar, punctuation, and usage. For any editor or writer, Strunk and White are a priceless combination; Strunk's precepts have become part of the American literary heritage, and White's "Approach to Style" is a classic. (More on Strunk is to be found in my appraisal of *Adios, Strunk and White,* just below.)

Hoffman, Gary and Glynis. *Adios, Strunk and White: A Handbook for the New Academic Essay.* 2d ed. Huntington Beach, Calif.: Verve Press, 1999. 240 pp.

Since Strunk and White's *Elements of Style* is useful to an editor trying to improve prose with a minimum of effort, perhaps we should consider why some successful practitioners are adiosing it. With wide-ranging metaphors daringly applied to advice about writing, the Hoffmans make headway against mundane rules and dull writing. Sections labeled "Splitting the Second," "Flashback," "Strip Tease," and "Raising the Dead" keep writers reading here. But since editors dare not apply raging imagination to their work, they'd better keep saying, "Buenos días, Professor Strunk."

"Strunk and White" has a million readers. Strunk's original essay is on the Web. With such circulation, even a clean little book has generated friction. So now we have *Adios, Strunk and White,* in a second edition, and a blurb for *Sin and Syntax* by Constance Hale (New York: Broadway Books, 1999): "Today's writers need more spunk than Strunk" (jacket copy). Fair enough.

Perhaps now is the time to quote from the "Introductory" to the original *Elements of Style*, where the not-so-staid professor concluded: "It is an old observation that the best writers sometimes disregard the rules of rhetoric. When they do so, however, the reader will usually find in the sentence some compensating merit, attained at the cost of the violation." So the "secrets of style" were to be found, Strunk said, beyond rules through "study of the masters of literature" (p. 6).

If I mention Professor William Strunk Jr. so respectfully, consider that writers and editors might well honor one of the soundest precepts to be found: *Omit needless words*. Yes, our best beloved dramatist played around with this notion. In *Hamlet*, Act 1, Scene 3, Ophelia tells her father that Hamlet proposed "love in honourable fashion,"

And hath given countenance to his speech, my lord,
With *almost* all the *holy* vows of heaven.

The italicized words appear in a Quarto edition, in which the plays were published early on, and are given authenticity by many scholars. But these unnecessary words are omitted in the First Folio. Good!

Yet hold on. Strunk, as consultant on Hollywood's *Romeo and Juliet*, declared (and thereby endeared himself to director George Cukor), that Shakespeare often preferred not to use two words for what he could say with style in ten:

Take thy fair hour Laertes; time be thine [Go now].

This combination of skills in the use of words we recognize as genius. And Strunk takes account of it.

Useful Pointers

Bernstein, Theodore. *Dos, Don'ts, and Maybes of English Usage*. New York: Gramercy, 1999. vi + 250 pp.

As usual with Bernstein, this book supports some old rules but questions others. Bernstein's *Careful Writer* and *Miss Thistlebottom's Hobgoblins* regrettably have slipped out of print.

Follett, Wilson. *Modern American Usage: A Guide.* Revised by Erik Wensberg. New York: Hill and Wang, 1998. xiii + 363 pp.

In this alphabetical listing of words and phrases, one finds much common sense and many neat points on style and usage, particularly on vogue words and tiresome words. The venerated earlier edition has been thoroughly updated. Lively substitutes are suggested for vague, timeworn, long-winded expressions, along with helpful comments on disappearing hyphens (the editor's hobgoblin). Wensberg has blasted *basically* off the page. The Appendix, "On Usage, Pedantry, Grammar and the Orderly Mind," is worth studying.

Harmon, Eleanor, and Ian Montagnes, eds. *The Thesis and the Book.* Toronto: University of Toronto Press, 1976. vii + 88 pp.

The author of a doctoral dissertation usually needs just the advice given here to produce a successful book, including guidance on what to get rid of and what to do with what is left. And pertaining to writing in general is general wisdom on having something to say, having perspective on it, and having an idea of the audience.

Wesson, Vann. *Generation X: A Field Guide and Lexicon.* San Diego: Orion Media, 1997. 200 pp.

Since most of us won't be editing a *cyberpunk* manuscript, we don't need to evaluate a book such as *Generation X*. But notice that the Cataloging-in-Publication Data of this book include in addition to "Humor" also the categories "Language" and "Dictionaries." So don't be surprised if *generic* one day turns up in dictionaries meaning also "really stupid; dull; out of it" (p. 76). Don't quiver when a youngster uses *scenic* to mean: "an event or occurrence that causes unwanted attention. 'Then Mona started screaming at the waiter for dropping her cheese sticks on the floor.' It was so scenic" (p. 146). This generation's talk is lively and to the point. These Xers are applying metaphors to life. That's what happens to the language.

Wilson, Kenneth G. *The Columbia Guide to Standard American English.* New York: Columbia University Press, 1993. xviii + 482 pp.

This indispensable guide for American editors gives welcome assistance to those who are struggling with new words, the changing meaning of old ones, added nuances for familiar phrases, and gradations of usage on the American social scene. It commences by stating that "because our language is constantly changing, mastering its appropriate usage is not a one-time task. . . . Instead we are constantly obliged to adjust, adapt, and revise what we have learned" (p. ix). And further: "This guide to Standard American usage tries to help you keep up with the new and keep track of the old" (p. xi). The advice on *fulsome* is good; the discussion of *plus* is neat; under *priest* we have a lead on avoiding sexual exclusion; under *buy* is a line on using good judgment. Thus with a pleasing preciseness editors are brought up to date and given reassuring authority.

REFERENCE WORKS

Biographical Names

Webster's New Biographical Dictionary. Springfield, Mass.: Merriam-Webster, 1995. xiii + 1,170 pp.

More than 30,000 individuals are listed. Editors will be grateful that possible end-of-line breaks are indicated. Living persons are not included.

Geographical Information

An editor occasionally needs to refer to a map and often needs to know the spelling of a place name.

Planet Earth: Macmillan World Atlas. New York: Macmillan, 1997. 416 pp.

In this extraordinarily beautiful volume with an index of 105,000 names, an editor should be able to find that elusive place name.

Webster's Geographical Dictionary. 3d ed. Springfield, Mass.: Merriam-Webster, 1997. 1,387 pp.

This new edition, with more than 47,000 entries and 252 maps, is a handy, authoritative reference.

Quotations

Editors would do well to verify all quotations from the Bible and from Shakespeare, for authors often think they know a passage and do not check back to these sources.

Bartlett, John. *Familiar Quotations: A Collection of Passages, Phrases, and Proverbs Traced to Their Sources in Ancient and Modern Literature.* 16th ed. Edited by Justin Kaplan. Boston: Little, Brown, 1992. lvi + 1,405 pp. 17th ed. announced for 2002.

This revised, updated edition of an old favorite contains over 20,000 quotations by over 2,550 authors, 340 of them new. Newcomers include Russell Baker, Leonard Bernstein, Mel Brooks, Elvis, Salman Rushdie, Dr. Seuss, and the Talmud. The index is organized by key words in the quotation.

Oxford Dictionary of Quotations. 5th ed. London: Oxford University Press, 1999. 1,152 pp.

The *Oxford* is a useful supplement to Bartlett.

Miscellaneous

Brewer's Dictionary of Phrase and Fable. 16th ed. New York: Harper Collins, 2000. 1,298 pp.

The Statesman's Year-Book. New York: St. Martin's. Published annually.

The World Almanac and Book of Facts. Mahwah, N.J.: World Almanac Books. Published annually.

Appendix
Figure 1. Sample of Computer-Edited Copy
(The "Redlined" Printout Also Showing Coding)

<h1>Qualifiers[1]

<USNOP>It is interesting to note that a{A}dverbs some times can cause trouble. Often when used to qualify a statement, or for extra emphasis, { or to qualify a statement,} you will find they are just so much extra bag{g}age that you will pay heavily for in loss of clarity and conciseness. Writers sometimes use {such }qualifiers to legitimis{z}e inexact statements. Upon o{O}ccasion{ally} qualifiers are justified, even necessary;{,} but to{o} often, they are a sign of mushy thought{thinking}.

TH{h}e use of apparentlyapparently can be dangerous, since it may encourage a writer to {draw a }conclude{sion} from lack of{insufficient} evidence: "Apparently Browning wrote them so well, he enjoyed writing dramatic monologues{, he wrote them so well}.{"}

The phrases{expressions}[501] for the most part, in essence, basically, fundamentally also must be classed as dangerous qualifiers--an aid to mushy thinking. They seem to take care of possible objections. If putting slang words within quotation marks is an attempt to pitch touch {pitch } without becoming defi led, the use of murky qualif{i}ei rs rates as an attempt to sound of{f} without suffering the consequences.

Obviously should be carefully watched. Consider whether the statement is so obvious that it had better be deleted.

Clearly also calls fore special vigilance. Like the direction "You can't miss it," clearly often portends a {cloudy }passage that is cloudy, though sometimes clearly is in a class with obviously and introduces an element that can well be omitted{.}

NOTE
<n>1. Taken and revised from Elsie Myers Stainton, Author and Editor at Work (Toronto: University of Toronto Press,[502] 1982), pp. 30-{3}1, 32-33.

----

501 Not all phrases.
502 No publishers given elsewhere.

If a word is to be deleted, ~~simply~~ cross it out with a line ~~through it~~, leaving it legible, although excised. If a word is to be added, insert a caret *in* the line and write the addition neatly ~~between~~ the line; (*above*) illegible editing is worse than none. To make a substitution, cross out what's there and write the ~~substitution~~ (*new word*) above the line, with a caret below. To move something ~~from one line to another~~, circle the part to be moved and connect it with an arrow to where it is to go. To delete a letter ~~from a word~~, strike it out and add arcs (har[ass]) to close the gap. To change a letter, obliterate it with a caret and add the desired letter above the caret (since[r]ity).

[margin note: to avoid it being ambiguous]

Call for capitals by three short lines under a letter, small capitals by two short lines (Trans World airlines or TWA). Indicate lowercase (lc) of a capital with a short slash through the [l]etter.

Indicate boldface by a neat wavy line. Underline words ~~that you want to be in~~ (*for*) italics. To delete italics, make a series of very short vertical lines through the underlining that indicates italics. ~~If you want~~ a numeral or abbreviation spelled out, circle it ((27), (U.S.)).

Mark note numbers in the text for superscript.

To move something ~~all the way~~ to the left margin (flush left) or ~~all the way~~ to the right margin (flush right), use an arrow pointing to a bracket at the appropriate margin.

Caspar, <u>A Word to the Wise</u> ———————→]

~~You can~~ use the margins to add ~~phrases~~ (*words*) with lines and a caret to show ~~exactly~~ where they are to go, ~~but~~ never write inserts vertically in the mar- (*sideways*) gins. If several lines must be added, type them on a new page, ~~giving it a~~ page number ~~such~~ (*it, for example,*) 17a, and on page 17 write "insert 17a," ~~indicating~~ with an arrow where ~~it~~ (*the insert*) goes.

Change a semicolon into a comma with a caret through the dot (⋀). Turn a colon or semicolon into a period with a circle through the upper dot (⊙). Change a comma to a period by drawing a circle around the comma⊙ To insert a period, add a circled dot⊙ Delete a comma⁄ with a delete sign through it.

Mark textual dashes, perhaps shown in the typing as two hyphens, with a one over an m (⅟M). Indicate shorter dashes, as between numbers or for compound words hyphenated, by a one over an n (4-17) and ⁄New York⁄Pennsylvania boundary line).

Check every hyphen that falls at the end of a line: if it is the hyphen in a compound word, double the hyphen into an equals sign, which tells the typesetter to retain it wherever it may fall (self=evident). If the hyphen marks only a break in a word happening to fall at the end of a line and would not be kept if the word was within a line, strike out the hyphen and indicate with arcs that the word is to be closed up (rose⁀wood) in all places where the compositor might have doubts.

Indicate needed space between words, lines, or paragraphs by two verticals through two horizontals (#) or by a simple slash (some⁀day). Indicate space to be closed up by arcs (copy⁀editor).

To transpose adjacent letters, words, or phrases, draw a boxy line that arches over one and under the other (reⓘⓥe). Both attention to detail and overall wariness are required of editors. They often need to either check a dictionary or style manual.

Footnote

1. Illustrated in this passage also are ways to avoid needless words.

Figure 3. Abbreviations for Notes and Bibliographies

app.	appendix
cf.	compare
ch.	chapter
ed.	edited, edition, editor
e.g.	for example
esp.	especially
et al.	and others
etc.	and so on, and so forth
ex. (exx.)	example(s)
f. (ff.)	page(s) following
ibid.	the same as the preceding reference
i.e.	that is
l. (ll.)	line(s)
MS	manuscript
n. (nn.)	note(s)
no.	number
n.p.	no place
n.s.	new series
p. (pp.)	page(s)
rev.	revised
sec.	section
v.	see, verse
viz.	namely
vol.	volume
vs.	versus

(Names of states and countries also may be abbreviated)

Figure 4. Signs for Correcting Proof

SIGN	MEANING	INSERTIONS IN TYPE LINES	MARGINAL CORRECTION
∧	Insert (sign in text only)	A go͜therd	a/
#	Space	sought͜to	#/
ℯ	Delete	bring ~~in~~ a	ℯ/
⌒	Close up	str⌒ay goat	⌒/
⌒̃	Delete & close up	bac⌒k to	⌒̃/
tr	Transpose (⎍ in text)	⌐flock│his⌐ He whis│led	tr/ tr/(whistled)
⌃;	Semicolon	in vain∧	⌃;/
⌃,	Comma	the goat∧straggling on∧	⌃,//
⊙	Period	paid no attention∧	⊙/
⦂	Colon	The boy threw a stone∧	⦂/
⌄	Apostrophe	it broke the goat∣s horn.	⌄/
⌃⌃ ⁗	Quotation marks (open & close)	∧Please do not tell the master,∧	⌃⌃ ⁗
lc	Lower-case (/ through letter)	Ⳇried the lad.	lc/
cap	Capital (⎓ under letter)	"you silly boy,"	cap/
/=/	Hyphen	the goat re∧	/=/
⊥M	Dash	plied∧the	⊥M ⁗
Ⓧ	Defective letter (circle letter)	hor⌒n)	Ⓧ
wf	Wrong font (circle letter)	Ⓦill	wf (will)
/	(Use slash to separate corrections in a line)	spek thⱤough/ i besilent∧	a/⌒̃/ℯ/cap/ #/⁗
ital	Italic type (underline text)	<u>From</u>	ital /
rom	Roman type (circle text)	(Aesop's)	rom/
sc	Small caps (⎓ under letter)	Fable<u>s</u>	sc/

145

Index